Training
Your Dog

Dominique De Vito

ANIMAL PLANET ♥ PET CARE LIBRARY

Training Your Dog
Project Team
Editor: Heather Russell-Revesz
Copy Editor: Joann Woy
Design concept: Leah Lococo Ltd., Stephanie Krautheim
Design layout: Stephanie Krautheim

T.F.H. Publications
President/CEO: Glen S. Axelrod
Executive Vice President: Mark E. Johnson
Publisher: Christopher T. Reggio
Production Manager: Kathy Bontz

T.F.H. Publications, Inc.
One TFH Plaza
Third and Union Avenues
Neptune City, NJ 07753

Discovery Communications, Inc. Book Development Team
Marjorie Kaplan, President, Animal Planet Media
Carol LeBlanc, Vice President, Licensing
Elizabeth Bakacs, Vice President, Creative Services
Brigid Ferraro, Director, Licensing
Peggy Ang, Director, Animal Planet Marketing
Caitlin Erb, Licensing Specialist

07 08 09 10 11   3 5 7 9 8 6 4 2
Printed and bound in China

Library of Congress Cataloging-in-Publication Data
Vito, Dominique De.
 Training your dog / Dominique De Vito.
    p. cm. — (Animal planet pet care library)
 Includes bibliographical references and index.
 ISBN-13: 978-0-7938-3773-1 (alk. paper) 1. Dogs—Training. I. Title.
 SF431.V58 2007
 636.7'0887—dc22
 2006028937

The Leader In Responsible Animal Care For Over 50 Years!®
www.tfh.com

Table of **Contents**

Chapter 1

Dogs Will Be Dogs:

Understanding Your Canine

Today, thankfully, pets really are part of the family. No longer does it seem normal, much less acceptable, to see a dog chained to a dog house by himself in a large yard. You're more likely to find today's family dog asleep in a specially made bed that might even have his initials embroidered on it. For the companion who gives unconditional love, this seems a minor luxury.

You may have noticed, however, that your four-legged canine member of the family just isn't getting the household rules, even though you think you've made them clear. Maybe he's still not housetrained, or he snarls when you ask him to get off your bed. Maybe he won't stop jumping up on your kids, or he barks incessantly at the back door. As you're trying to read this book—or do anything quietly—your dog may be pestering you to play with him, making it nearly impossible to ignore him.

The flip side of the "love" coin, where dogs are concerned, is that no matter how wonderful they are, they are still dogs. And dogs will be dogs, like it or not, take it or leave it. (Please, don't leave it; don't condemn your dog because he does doggy things.)

What Is a Dog?

It may seem like a silly question, but have you ever thought about it? What makes a dog a dog? What makes a Great Dane and a Chihuahua—two very different kinds of dogs—the same species? What defines a dog as a dog?

Scientifically speaking, the dog is from the kingdom Animalia; the phylum Chordata; the subphylum Vertebrata; the class Mammalia; the order Carnivora; the family Canidae; the genus *Canis*; the species *lupus*; and the subspecies *familiaris*. The full scientific name is *Canis lupus familiaris*. The *American Heritage Dictionary* defines a dog (n) as: "A domesticated carnivorous mammal *(Canis familiaris)*

The full scientific name for the dog is Canis lupus familiaris.

related to the foxes and wolves and raised in a wide variety of breeds."

It's true: The Fidos we know and love are descendents of wolves. But how did *Canis lupus familiaris* come to differentiate itself not just from its wolf, fox, and coyote cousins, but into the large variety of what we know as individual breeds? Many dog books reach into the campfires of our ancestors for stories of how our kind learned to hunt from their kind and, over time, developed a symbiotic relationship that eventually led to their kind wanting to hang around our kind. Essentially, from the time of the first cave-raised wolf pups to the proliferation of the several hundred distinct breeds of dogs recognized around the world today, a whole lot of domesticating was going on.

It's amazing to think that over the course of several thousand years—and in some cases mere decades—dog breeds have become so varied and so distinct. As for thinking of Aunt Judy's Pekingese as part wolf, it's fair to say that a genetically refined, domesticated dog is not a wolf, just as today's humans have little in common with their caveman ancestors, although the fact remains that the direct connection exists. Perhaps there's some truth in

The Expert Knows

Dogs Can Be Dogs

Because they share the same DNA, all breeds of dogs can mate with all other breeds of dogs. With the technology that makes artificial insemination possible, almost any combination is imaginable. If today's trend is "doodle" dogs (Labradoodle, Goldendoodle, etc.), who share Poodle bloodstock, perhaps tomorrow's trend will be Dane dogs, in which the Great Dane is a significant contributor. Wonder what a Cockadane would look like?

the saying, "You can take the dog out of the wolf, but you can't take the wolf out of the dog."

Understanding Dogs

With a clearer definition of what constitutes a dog, understanding that animal then becomes easier. A dog not only likes to but needs to chew. A dog is a social animal, preferring to live in packs rather than alone. A dog is an omnivore, able to eat meat and vegetables, although he is better sustained with a meat-based protein source.

Dogs communicate in many ways different from ours. Sure, they bark to express themselves, but they also get a

SENIOR DOG TIP

Mixed Breeds

If you adopted an older dog—particularly if the dog is a mix that you can't quite pinpoint—you face a greater challenge in working with the nature–nurture thing, because you may never know enough about either his breed or his upbringing. If this is the case, all you can do is your best. As you get to know your dog, you'll learn to work with certain character traits; certainly, he will be doing the same with you. Think patience, praise, and persistence, and hold on to your sense of humor.

Nature *and* Nurture

Your dog's behavior is a product of his nature—what he was born with as a dog and as a pure or mixed breed—and nurture—what is provided him by his environment.

What Your Dog Is Born With (Nature)

If you fall in love with a Pug, and you live on a house on a hill in the desert, with lots of steps to go up and down and daytime temperatures that top 80°F (26.6°C) regularly, you will need to carry your dog up and down those steps in the daytime; provide him loads of fresh, cool water; and keep the air conditioning on. A Pug's short nose—a natural, genetic trait—makes him fairly intolerant of extremes of temperature

whole lot more information from their noses than we do, which is why they sniff so intently, whether it's a tasty treat, someone new coming into the house, or the urine or feces of another dog or animal. Breeds of dogs were developed to perform certain tasks, and those characteristics help define who they are, whether those characteristics mesh with our lifestyle or not.

Your dog's behavior is a product of nature and nurture.

or physical exercise. He simply can't breathe well enough to tolerate them for long. If you know this about Pugs, and are willing to accommodate their very real physical needs, then you can make the dog's life more comfortable and greater peace will reign in your household.

If you fall in love with a Labrador Retriever, on the other hand, you must accept that he will need several long walks a day, and this still may not accommodate his physical and exuberant nature. A young Labrador Retriever (and many older ones) will fetch a ball or stick that you throw in the water for as long as you can stand doing it, then want to keep playing fetch on land. He will bring you the ball over and over again, and will seemingly never tire of the game. You will be completely worn out, and he will be getting warmed up. How will a dog like this handle being left alone in a confining crate while everyone is at work, school, soccer games, or barbecues with family?

The nature of your particular breed can be discovered through speaking with those who have been its caretaker for years. Maybe your neighbor has had Irish Setters or Maltese. Books on particular breeds abound, and are excellent resources. Certainly the dog's breeder should know about your breed's characteristics. Groups that "rescue" a particular breed and help those dogs find new homes are

The Same, but Different

The wonderful thing about purebreds is that they definitely share characteristics. It is safe to generalize that all Dachshunds, for example, enjoy a good dig, since they were bred to go to ground and go after vermin. But it's also true that every dog is an individual. If you have a Dalmatian who doesn't want to run, or a Sheltie who doesn't like to bark, it's no mystery, it's just your dog.

excellent sources of information about breed traits—particularly those that may have contributed to a dog being abandoned in the first place.

You want to learn as much as you can about the nature of your beast because it will help you tremendously in understanding how best to train him. A hound needs a different approach than a dog from a herding breed, and even a scenthound will vary from a sighthound in how he responds to his world. If you want to be Number One in your dog's world so that he respects and listens to you, you must be able to imagine the world from his point of view.

What You Contribute (Nurture)

Just as determining the physical capabilities of your breed is important in understanding what he's all about, assessing what you will provide through your family situation and environment—the nurture part of the equation—is vital, as well. Going back to the examples of the Pug and the Lab given earlier, living in a hot place or needing to confine your young dog are both environmental factors that you contribute and, ultimately, control. Some others are:

MAKE IT EASY!

Understanding Dogs

- Research your breed to find out his general characteristics.

- Be aware of your dog's nature, as well as how his environment affects him.

- If you feel stuck, professional help is but a click or a phone call away through the Association of Pet Dog Trainers (APDT), at www.apdt.com, or 1-800-PET-DOGS.

- **Family size and makeup.** Are you retired and single? A recent empty nester? A new grandparent who anticipates a fair share of babysitting? A recent high school or college graduate? A couple just starting a family? A household with grown children? Are you a workaholic with little free time? Are your children very young, just starting to date, or overscheduled? The number of adults and children in your house on a regular basis, as well as the kind of people you are, will affect your dog.

- **Where you live.** Is your home an apartment in the city? A farm with lots of acreage? A place where it's typically warm, or where you can expect harsh winters?

- **How you live.** Would you describe yourself as a neat freak? Do you like to go out a lot, or do you travel frequently? Do you have a fenced-in yard? Are you OK with a doggy digging area in your garden?

- **How are you as a trainer or coach?** Do you feel you are patient, consistent, goal-oriented? Or are you impulsive, unpredictable, or quick to offend? Your own way of dealing with the world and those around you will affect how you train your dog. Acknowledge your strengths and weaknesses, and factor them into your expectations.

Training Is a Holistic Thing

Now that you understand your dog a

Good, Better, Best

Sure, it would be nice if we could all offer our dogs unlimited room to run and explore, our undivided attention when they wanted it, the very best food fed several times a day, and children as reliably predictable companions, but none of that is reality. What is realistic is to be aware of the elements of your environment and how they fit or don't fit your dog's needs, and accommodate and compromise to ensure everyone's safety and well-being.

Where kids are concerned, if you haven't gotten a dog yet, re-evaluate what breed might be best for the kind of children you have. If you have a dog, and things don't seem to be going so well, talk to your kids about their behaviors that will minimize your dog's less desirable traits and maximize those you want or like.

humans are complex creatures. We are all functioning in environments loaded with subtle influences, from how things are going at work to what the temperature is outside to how well we sleep, what we eat, and what our individual body chemistry is. The time of day you train your dog, when and what he's eaten before you train, who else is around—and so much more— can and will affect your dog's ability to respond and learn (as well as your ability to focus and teach!).

This book has been written to help you minimize the distracting influences and keep your training positive and productive. Your dog will forgive your minor mistakes—remember to forgive him his. Appreciate what you accomplish together, and don't expect miracles. Enjoy your dog, and be proud of the fact that you're trying your best.

11

Understanding Your Canine

little better, it's easy to see that you can't simply "program" your dog to be obedient. Commands don't come out of thin air, to be learned and complied with. Dogs are complex creatures;

Chapter 2

The Foundations for

Successful Training

When your dog is a puppy, it seems like you have all the time in the world to teach him right from wrong. You figure "lessons" can wait while you simply get to know each other, which involves a lot of petting, playing, giving treats "just because," letting the puppy get away with jumping on the furniture, and so forth.

Patience and positive energy help shape the dog of your dreams.

Of course, your puppy is adorable and, of course, you want to shower him with love. No argument there. But think about what your puppy is learning from your behavior: You are a bottomless source of all the things he wants. Well, what happens when what he wants isn't so cute, and you aren't happy about it? You're upset, he's upset, things become confusing. Confusion leads to anxiety, anxiety leads to poor behavior—next thing you know, you've created a monster.

The same scenario can play itself out if an older dog joins your household. Even a dog who's been trained to understand the basics may err in his ways when he goes through the transition of joining a new family— especially when the family forgives certain behaviors because they want to be nice to the new dog. This is perfectly understandable, and part of the whole process of getting to know each other.

The perfect time to begin incorporating manners-oriented lessons into your everyday interactions is during that time when you and your puppy (or dog) are madly in love with each other and think neither can do any wrong. With time on your side, and lots of positive energy, you can begin to shape the dog of your dreams.

However, no matter how ready you may be to start training your dog, if you don't have the proper tools—the right equipment, ideas about when best to train, and even the proper mindset—your efforts won't get you what you're looking for. In fact, four elements directly contribute to your success:

1. Defining good manners
2. The proper equipment
3. Incorporating training time into your dog's (and family's) normal routine
4. Having the right attitude

Defining Good Manners

How would the dog of your dreams behave? Would he sit to greet visitors at the door? Would he go to his bed when you asked? Would he do fun tricks when requested, like shake, speak, or roll over? Would he wait politely at the door while you got ready to go for a walk? Would he listen when you said "Leave it," "Off," or "Drop it"?

A well-mannered dog should be able

When Puppy Can Do No Wrong

It doesn't matter what the breed or mix of breed is: Every young puppy is adorable and irresistible. Who cares if they scamper around the house at 100 miles an hour and almost trip you when you come home? So he has a few accidents— they're small and easily cleaned up. His pathetic crying at night always stops when you bring him into bed with you, so what's the harm? You're both happier that way. Ah, the honeymoon stage. Just beware that habits are forming from your puppy's first moments in your home that will carry over into adulthood.

to do all these things—and much more. They truly aren't that much to ask of a family member. The reward, too, is that your dog will be appreciated by everyone in the family (including the non-dog-loving members) and by guests. This will make for a home where cooperation and peace prevail over sharp demands and the stress of punishment or even isolation for your dog.

Another point worth considering when defining good manners is what your own expectations are. Manners training does yield an obedient dog— one who listens and complies with requests for certain behaviors. However, a dog is a dog, just as people are people. You can't expect your dog to be perfect. You can't expect your dog to "get it" right away and remember what you taught when you next ask him to do it 2 weeks later. Being obedient doesn't mean being robotic, just as teaching your dog doesn't mean punishing him into submission. A dog (or a child, spouse, or coworker) will more willingly comply when they feel rewarded and appreciated for their efforts.

By the way, nothing is worse than working hard on something and having your time and achievements undermined by someone who comes along and even unknowingly does something to set all your work back. This can and does happen in dog training when one person goes it alone in a family. You may have your dog responding like a soldier at drill camp, dropping to a sit or a down on the first (and only) request. Then your 5-year-old comes along and say "Sit, sit, sit, SIT, siiiittt" until your dog is not even listening or responding to the word. Or your spouse will give a treat before asking your dog to do anything. In these cases, you'll quickly be the one growling at your pack. To avoid this, bring them into the game plan. Show them how you want to work with the dog and have them participate. You'll all do much better together.

What Makes a Well-Mannered Dog?

For everything that you may teach your puppy or dog to do as you grow together, you must rely on the solid foundation of these seven things:

1. Socialization
2. Housetraining
3. Sit
4. Down
5. Stay
6. Come
7. Walk Nicely on Leash

Define good manners before you start training your dog.

The idea is to make training your dog easy and practical. After all, lessons that are short, fun, and get positive results are easier and more achievable than those that you feel obligated to give, don't really understand, and don't ultimately get you what you want. By teaching your puppy or dog a handful of basic requests—*as you go about your regular routine*—slowly but surely you will have a well-mannered, obedient dog. We'll discuss how to teach the seven foundation behaviors in later chapters.

Proper Equipment

If you've been to a pet supply store recently, you realize how much stuff is available to help you train your dog. How do you choose what's appropriate for your dog and your purposes? Before you find yourself feeling dazed by the selection at the store, give some thought to your situation and make some notes. The things you need should be targeted to your dog's size and energy level, and they should be easy to use and care for.

Some people think that training equipment can—and should—form an association on the part of the dog so

The Expert Knows

Consider Your Dog

Do you have a 100-pound (45 kg) Alaskan Malamute or a 10-pound (4.5 kg) Shih Tzu? A 60-pound (27 kg) Dalmatian or a 20-pound (9 kg) Dachshund? When you go out, is your dog's energy so great that you think he could pull a wagon full of kids down the street, or is he content to plod along with little assistance or direction from you? Whatever your situation, you have probably gotten equipment that you feel relates to your dog's size and energy level—and hopefully it's working! When it comes to training your dog, though, you may need to reassess what you're using.

that when you bring it out the dog understands that you're going to be working together. Just as athletes wear clothes specific to their activity, so your dog should wear gear specific to training. If you want to go beyond manners training with your dog, you may get to the point at which you need specific equipment for a specific activity. For manners training, though, your dog should associate your requests with the regular routine of his day.

The Crate

Crates are a great idea for your dog—they are wonderful tools for housetraining, and they give your dog a space of his own. Several types of

Lose the Bling

If your dog normally wears a dainty rhinestone-encrusted collar, or a rolled leather collar, or something more decorative than practical, you should consider replacing it with the basic training collar, at least for a while. Because even basic collars are fairly fashion-oriented these days, you can still find one that complements your dog's personality and gives him the "look" you want while being effective for training.

crates are available to choose from—heavy-duty plastic ones that are often suitable for airline travel and can even be folded when not in use; folding wire mesh crates; even soft-sided ones convenient for transporting your dog.

To choose one that's best for you and your dog, consider your circumstances. Do you have a small- or medium-sized dog with whom you want to travel frequently? You may need a strong cart for the car and a more flexible cart for a hotel room or guest room. Folding wire mesh crates are better looking than the large, hard plastic crates and tend to be less obtrusive when set up in the kitchen or family room. You can put a sheet over them to give your dog more privacy.

Something you may want to consider is a foldable crate or carrier.

These are handy because they can be easily dismantled when not in use, whether it's because you want to carry the crate into another room for your dog, or because you want to put the crate away while you entertain.

The Collar

Whatever collar your dog is currently wearing may be fine to use when training him, or it may not be. Not too long ago nearly everyone agreed that dogs should be trained in what some call a "choke chain" collar. It's a metal link collar with two circles on the end.

The collar goes around your dog's neck in such a way that, when you need to apply pressure, it "chokes" your dog, causing him to pull up short. Theoretically, this turns his attention to you.

The thinking on the effectiveness of this collar has changed, however, and today most trainers agree that basic manners training should be done with the dog wearing a flat buckle (or snap) collar. This kind of collar is made out of leather, nylon, or cotton, and closes with a buckle or a plastic snap. This all-purpose collar usually has a couple of metal loops on it—one for tags, and one for the leash to attach to. These collars come in different lengths and different widths (as well as many colors and styles). They are simple to get on and off, reliable, washable, and durable. Larger, stronger dogs, and even medium-sized dogs, need widths of 1 inch (2.5 cm) or more. Toy dogs, on the other hand, shouldn't have that much weight around their necks, and can go with the .5-inch (1.3 cm) widths. Determine the proper length for your dog by measuring around his neck.

Leashes

Yes, leashes. Even basic training requires a couple of different-sized leashes. Two leashes should do it; three may be the ideal

A flat buckle collar is best for training.

number for you. Again, this depends on the size of your dog. For all dogs, you'll need one 4- to 6-foot (1.2- to 1.8-m) long leash for the majority of your training, and one 12-foot (3.6-m) cotton leash for distance training (particularly for training "Come"). If you have a medium to large dog, consider getting a short leash that looks like and serves as a handle. It's something your dog can wear around the house without dragging, and it makes getting a hold of him for reminders really easy.

Do not use retractable or chain leashes to train your dog. Retractable leashes take some getting used to and can also hurt you or your dog if you get tangled up in the line. Chain leashes are distracting because of the noise they make, and they can also hurt your hands should your dog jerk or lunge while you're working with him.

Training Treats

The training methodology presented in this book is basic reward training, and the reward is usually treats. When you think of getting a treat for doing something right, you may think of anything from candy to chips to ice cream— something worth working for!

Training treats should be small and easy to eat.

This concept is true for your dog, too. But it's easy to see how your friend could pack on the pounds if you overdid the treats or gave too many of the wrong kind.

The thing about treats is that you will need a lot of them to reward your dog's correct behavior. You should also vary the treats so you keep him interested. And, because you'll be training your dog in all parts of the house, you'll want to keep different kinds of treats in different containers in different places. Wow, that's a lot to think about!

The "normal" treat trainers recommend is something soft and smelly that is quickly and easily ingested by your dog. Not something he needs to take time to chew or wants to run off and chew somewhere else—something instantly edible and gratifying. For most dogs, the foods that best fit the bill are slices of hot dog that are then quartered so the pieces are the size of peas; pieces of hard cheese or string cheese also cut up into pea-sized pieces; or similarly small pieces of cooked meat, cold cuts, or prepared dog food that comes in sausage shapes. These are considered "high impact" treats and should be used when introducing a new request.

While a request is in the learning stages, and when it needs to be reinforced, you can choose a treat that's less perishable and stinky. Small treats you can put in lidded

Treat Bags

Treats can be stored in glass or plastic lidded containers, but how do you work with wet, stinky stuff like meat and cheese? You can buy a "goody pouch" that you wear like a fanny pack. It allows you to work with both hands, and it keeps the treats protected. Another option is to use a small, strong plastic bag that can go in a coat pocket or even the pockets of your jeans or shorts. Another option is to take only a small handful of treats at a time and come back for a refill if you need to. Experiment to see what method you're most comfortable with.

containers around the house include bite-sized, whole-grain breakfast cereals (like Cheerios), kibble (as long as it's in small pieces), fresh popcorn, or even baby carrot sticks (keep these in the fridge). Don't use fatty snack food or sugary cereals. Remember that your dog's treats are part of his overall calorie intake for the day. If you're doing several training sessions a day and using hot dogs or cheese, you may want to cut back some on the amount of kibble or wet food you give your dog for the day.

Making Time for Training

Whether your dog is still a puppy or is an older dog, he will be better behaved and more manageable if you put him on a regular schedule. Consider the schedule another training tool, as necessary as a collar and leash. Dogs, like most of us, thrive on routine.

Dogs are fairly predictable. They need to eat, sleep, be taken outside or to a designated spot to relieve themselves, go for walks and exercise, and interact with others. The primary influences on your schedule will be when your dog needs to go outside and when he eats. These things depend partly on his age and partly on his temperament. The following is a typical schedule for a puppy, but it is easily transferable to an older dog, especially one you may have acquired recently, for whom it's important to establish a new (and lasting) routine.

Setting up a schedule is an essential part of training.

Older Dog Attitudes

Think about your expectations for your older dog, whether he's been with you from puppyhood or not. Keep in mind that just because he's on in years doesn't mean he should know better or that he's necessarily learned what something means. He may associate your body language or the time of day with something he normally does without having any sense of what you're really asking of him. It's best to start everything you want to teach from the basis of your dog not knowing.

Setting Up a Schedule

Young puppies must go outside or "do their business" as soon as they get up in the morning, so be ready! If your bundle of fluff wakes you at 6:00 AM whining and possibly circling, it's time to get him out! Do not expect a young puppy to adjust to your normal time of getting up. For now, you must take care of him first. Same goes for an older dog—so, if he's giving you signals, don't delay.

After relieving himself, your puppy will be hungry, and your older dog will expect to eat. He'll need to go outside again soon after eating. When those needs are met, he'll move on to wanting to chew, play, go for a walk, and do other doggy things.

A typical schedule for a young puppy whose family is gone most of the day might look like this:

6:00 am Take puppy out to relieve himself

6:15 am Feed first meal

6:30 am Take puppy back outside to relieve himself

6:40 am Give puppy attention through play, grooming, etc.

7:00 am Confine puppy while taking care of self or children

7:30/8:00 am Take puppy out

8:00 am Confine puppy while you or you and children are gone

11:30/12:00 pm Take puppy out to relieve himself

12:00 pm Feed puppy second meal

12:15 pm Take puppy back outside to relieve himself

12:30 pm Confine puppy if leaving the house again

3:00 pm Take puppy out when children are home from school

3:15 pm Feed puppy a nutritious snack

3:30 pm Take puppy out again

3:45-5:00 pm Interact with puppy as appropriate. This is a good time for some basic training, socializing, going for walks around the neighborhood,

23

playing, or supervised time in the rest of the house. Take time for potty breaks.

5:30 pm Take puppy out then feed third meal

5:45 pm Take puppy out again

6:00–8:00 pm Supervised play, exercise, and training time with family

Before your bedtime: Take puppy out

At bedtime: Confine puppy to sleeping area

For Puppy Owners

If this seems like a lot of work, it is! However, the better able you are to stick to this kind of schedule, the more quickly your puppy will be housetrained, and the faster you'll find him settling into the family routine. If getting home to care for the puppy around mid day is impossible for you, find and set up an arrangement with a local pet-sitting or pet-walking service to come in and take care of your puppy. It is inhumane to leave a young puppy (or even an older dog) alone for more than a few hours at a time, and you certainly can't expect a baby puppy not to have accidents in the house if he can't get out to relieve himself.

For Owners of Older Dogs

Review this schedule and see where you can modify it to suit your dog. You won't need to worry about the afternoon feeding and, if your dog is housetrained, he won't need to go out

as often (although owners who are gone for longer than 7 hours at a time should invest in a dog walker for the health and sanity of their dog).

Fitting in Training

Once you have a schedule or routine established with your puppy or dog, you'll find there are many opportunities to fit in training time. The methods described in this book take

FAMILY-FRIENDLY TIP

Get the Family Involved

Chances are likely that you'll be successful with the training and feel pretty darn good about what you're accomplishing with your dog. This will be noticed by your kids, spouse, and anyone else who sees you training your dog. They will probably think what you're doing looks like fun and want to join in. Welcome their interest. Even a 4-year-old can hold a treat for a dog and ask him to sit for it (with your help, at first). Even a tired spouse can "train" the dog from the comfort of a recliner if he or she has a handful of popcorn and some commercial time.

Staying positive increases the bond with your dog.

only a few seconds at a time to teach and should only be repeated a few times during any training "session." The idea is that you should work on basic requests (training) at all times during the day and in situations that are part of your and your dog's normal day.

For example, the time just before breakfast is a great time to work on Sit, Down, and Stay. Your dog's hunger will motivate him toward the treats, and your goal is for him to learn to sit and stay before you put his food bowl down for him anyway. Another great time to train is when the family is watching TV at night. While sharing a bowl of popcorn, you can ask your dog to Sit (popcorn reward), Down

(popcorn reward), Stay (popcorn reward)—even Down/Stay on the other side of the room, then Come! (Several popcorn rewards.)

When training is fun and constructive, and really takes very little additional time, it'll be something the whole family can understand and participate in, making it that much more successful for all of you.

Attitude—The Power of Positive Thinking

Sure, it's a cliché, and maybe you don't think of yourself as a positive person, so you're wondering if you're doomed to fail. Not to worry! You don't have to be Mr. or Mrs. Sunshine to earn the

Make training a part of your daily routine.

process, have a sense of how you'd like your dog to behave, have invested in the equipment, and have established a schedule, the only thing left is to read about how to do the training and get going. Believe me, when your dog learns that you will be giving him little pieces of hot dog for doing something as simple (to him) as lowering his backside to the floor, he'll be eager to repeat that for you. The great thing about the training methods in this book is that you rarely have to put your hands on your dog to have him do what you want. Let your treats do the work for you—that element alone keeps the training positive in the mind of your dog.

Expectations

Regarding expectations, keep them simple and achievable—always. If you amaze yourself by how quickly your dog learns something, you may want to up the ante too quickly and immediately introduce another request. Don't! Repeat, praise, repeat, praise, for

respect and cooperation of your dog so that you are both successful with the training. You do, however, need to be realistic about your expectations, aware of your own moods and how your dog is responding, able to end training time if a session is not going well, and enthusiastic enough to want to practice and involve the other members of your family.

If you are committed to this

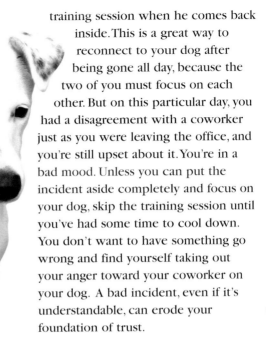

training session when he comes back inside. This is a great way to reconnect to your dog after being gone all day, because the two of you must focus on each other. But on this particular day, you had a disagreement with a coworker just as you were leaving the office, and you're still upset about it. You're in a bad mood. Unless you can put the incident aside completely and focus on your dog, skip the training session until you've had some time to cool down. You don't want to have something go wrong and find yourself taking out your anger toward your coworker on your dog. A bad incident, even if it's understandable, can erode your foundation of trust.

as long as a week at a time when learning something new— even longer for something more complicated. Be amazed, then let it go, and be amazed again a little while later. That will keep the training on track for you, because you and your dog will be constantly "winning."

Say you've established a routine with your dog so that, when you come home from work, you let him out first thing, get a few treats, and have a mini-

MAKE IT EASY!

Training

Make training easy and fun by:

- Defining good manners and deciding how you want your dog to behave.
- Choosing the proper training equipment for your dog's size and training goals.
- Making time for training by setting up a routine.
- Staying positive and keeping your dog's trust.

Chapter 3

Nice to Meet You!

Socialization and Your Dog

What if you lived with a family that never went out and did anything with other people? Yours was a loving family, and everyone was happy, but you didn't go to school with other kids, you didn't go to the movies, you didn't play sports—you basically lived in a bubble. How scary it would be for you to eventually run into other people—loud people, rough people, old people, all types. What if, all of a sudden, a bunch of them came to your house? Would you hide, run away, try to protect your family?

This may be an unimaginable scenario for most of us, but that's what it's like for a puppy growing into a dog and living with a family who never exposes him to other people, places, or animals. Your dog is friendly and nice with you because he trusts you. Why should he trust other people or other dogs he doesn't know? Why should he know how to behave if you suddenly go somewhere together, like to a hotel or to a friend's house, particularly if your visit involves leaving him alone for any amount of time?

For the emotional health of your puppy and your soon-to-be adult dog—as well as his physical safety and that of your family—it is critical to get him out into the world where he can meet and experience as many kinds of people, other animals, and environments as possible. It's called *socialization*, and every positive interaction will boost his self-confidence and make him less afraid. It will expose him to safe situations. And to unsafe situations, where you will be there to assure or to rescue him so that he can better handle all other experiences.

Puppy Socialization

Thank goodness we live at a time when dog-knowledgeable folks agree that puppies can get out into the world a lot sooner than was once believed acceptable. Until they've had all their

Socializing your puppy is critical for his development.

shots, they're not completely immune from some serious diseases, but if you ask visitors to wash their hands when they handle your "baby," and you are careful to avoid unclean areas in your neighborhood, even a 6- or 7-week-old puppy should be just fine.

Keep It Positive

Before you start, keep in mind that the new people and experiences you are exposing your puppy to must be positive. Because dogs are individuals and are each sensitive in their own ways, you must be a real protector and leader of your best friend. Don't put him in danger by encouraging him to "sniff" another dog who seems aggressive. Don't let a group of kids have their way with your puppy. Don't turn him loose in a dog run before taking a look at the other dogs to make sure they're not too boisterous. Don't leave him alone in a strange place for long until he's comfortable with even short absences. Use common sense and your own sensitivity to expose him in as positive and beneficial a way as possible to the wonders of the world.

Where to Socialize

Great places to socialize your puppy include playgrounds, shopping centers, the streets of your town—anywhere you'll find a large variety of friendly folks.

Supervise interactions between your puppy and children.

Socialization With People

He thinks nothing is better than humans giving him treats, so take him out and ask kind strangers (and of course, friends, neighbors, co-workers, and others you trust) to say his name and give him a tasty treat. This teaches him that strange-looking giants looming over him are usually friendly and, in fact, often give him yummy stuff.

With safety in mind, taking your dog as many places as possible with you is a terrific way to socialize him. Mall parking lots, national parks, children's sporting events or practices, the local downtown shopping area—all are

FAMILY-FRIENDLY TIP

Your Family and Your Puppy

If young children aren't told what to expect from puppies, they can feel hurt or disappointed when the object of their affection nips or pounces on them. These negative feelings can escalate, making everyone unhappy—including the puppy, who is bound to be isolated. Explaining the pup's behavior will help, and don't be too lenient with the puppy, either. Rowdy puppies must be confined until they calm down. An excellent book to read on the subject is Raising Puppies & Kids Together: A Guide for Parents by Pia Silvani and Lynn Eckhardt.

should be easy—they are naturally attracted to each other. The problem is that neither young puppies nor young children have developed much self control, and their enthusiasm sometimes gets them into trouble. Puppies have razor-sharp teeth and use their mouths to explore *everything*. Children similarly use their hands to explore *everything*. Puppy teeth meeting small, sensitive hands often results in the child's flesh being pinched, which causes them to flinch and cry out, which may further excite the puppy. This may lead to a very unpleasant experience for everyone.

It's your responsibility to supervise the interactions of your puppy and any children he meets (including your own). Before being allowed to pet and play with your puppy, explain certain rules they need to follow and things they need to know about your puppy. These should include:

- Sit or kneel while playing with the puppy so the dog isn't picked up and dropped (even an innocent accident can really hurt the puppy).
- Pet the puppy calmly so he doesn't get too excited.
- Be gentle with the puppy.
- If the puppy starts biting at you, put your hands behind your back and turn your face away while I get him away from you. Getting upset will make the puppy nervous.
- If the puppy nips your hand, make

places where you'll encounter all sorts of folks and a variety of circumstances. These outings will also give you clues about what may trigger your dog to react defensively or abnormally. Take note and work to desensitize your dog to these hot spots.

Socialization With Children

Introducing your puppy to children

Puppy kindergarten is a great way to socialize your pup.

the sound of a dog in distress and make your hand into a fist to protect your fingers.

Socialization With Other Dogs

An excellent venue in which to expose pups to other people and dogs is a puppy kindergarten class. Kindergartens are now offered by most trainers in conjunction with their regular classes for older dogs. Puppy kindergarten is a supervised space of puppy playtime, where you can see how your friend interacts with others and vice versa. Learning this about him will help tremendously in setting realistic training goals. If he's the "wallflower" type, you must be extra-sensitive in how you respond to him. If he's the class clown, he may need a firmer hand. Before enrolling, ask if you can watch a class. Pay attention to how the trainer handles the group. If you think the pups are a bit wild, or it looks like some puppy "bullies" are present, discuss your concerns with the instructor. Also, discuss your pup's characteristics with the trainer so she will know something about your dog before he joins the class.

If you have an older puppy or can't find a puppy kindergarten class, your puppy can meet and play with lots of other dogs. You probably already know some of the dogs in your neighborhood. Think about their personalities, and only introduce your pup to those you think are nice. When dogs meet for the first time, they sniff and circle actively, and sometimes the more submissive dog will lie down and expose his belly. It's tough to determine sometimes if the behavior you see is normal dog behavior or if it's something that will turn aggressive. Keep both dogs on a loose leash, and let them figure it out as much as possible.

Allow your dog to meet other well-behaved dogs.

Dog parks can be wonderful or menacing; it's up to you to make sure it's the former for your dog and not the latter. If it looks like some bigger, tougher dogs have formed a "pack" and are chasing other dogs down, you probably shouldn't bring your puppy into the mix. If the dogs appear to be under control, and their people are paying attention to them (as well as socializing with each other, which is typical), then your puppy should be fine. Use common sense and your best judgment.

Socialization with Other Animals

Your puppy must meet other kinds of animals, too. Cats, horses, ferrets, reptiles—if you already have any of these as a pet, or if you bring another animal home, introductions need to be made. Always keep your puppy on a short leash when introducing him to strange animals. Be sure that the other animal is basically friendly, and give it the space it needs to feel safe. Approach a horse slowly, letting your pup and the horse sniff each other. If the cat or ferret were in your house first, they will approach your pup in due time. Encourage a positive meeting by having a tasty treat ready for any animal who says hello nicely. Keep your pup on his leash, and praise him for "accepting" the other animal. Take him away from the other animal if he gets overly excited. Confine him to another room or a crate, and go to your other pet and reassure him that you are not upset with him, but with the puppy. Sometimes these things take time, but eventually they typically work out.

Introducing Strange Objects

Your puppy may find lots of things frightening or startling in your home, including vacuum cleaners, blenders,

SENIOR DOG TIP

Socializing

Your senior citizen will slow down as he ages, often almost imperceptibly. Dogs that are used to tearing around the park with their buddies may start to stumble around certain turns. They may lose their enthusiasm for leaping at toys. They may begin to feel vulnerable around dogs who are more physically fit, and this may result in some surprisingly antisocial or even aggressive behavior, which may lead to your leaving him home more often—the opposite of a healthy social life.

When you notice any of these things, first get a complete physical check-up from your veterinarian. Discuss which supplements or medications may help your dog's body and emotions. The bottom line is: He doesn't want to miss out on any of his normal routine. Help him stay connected and involved by paying attention to what he needs.

Socializing an older dog takes time and patience

object. When he appears comfortable with the object, do something with it—turn a blender on low speed, turn on the vacuum, open a paper bag. Your pup may startle, but then return to explore. Stay calm and encouraging, and give treats for further exploration. Remember, slow and steady—and reward for acceptance.

To help your dog feel safe when you're not at home, leave a radio on programmed to a classical music station (but not too loud). The music can soothe your dog. Have a bag of treats in your pocket when you're walking your dog, and let him explore parked trucks and cars, rewarding him for trying. Take him to a fire or police station and ask if he can explore.

If you pay attention to what could frighten your pup; do everything you can to make the world a positive, safe place for him; and expose him to strange things in moderation, he should grow to be accepting of whatever you accept.

Adult Dogs and Socialization

You'll know your adult dog has missed out on some critical socializing if he's

floor grates, the sound of children running up and down the stairs, or particularly loud noises from the TV. Puppies left alone for part of the day may become scared by things they hear outside, like trucks, sirens, or your neighbor slamming his door. These are all things puppies must be socialized to as well, so they aren't always afraid of them. How to do it?

For objects that make noise, allow your pup to sniff them when they're off. Give him treats as he sniffs the overly protective or afraid, or he's awkward with other dogs. This doesn't mean the situation is hopeless, but it does mean you have your work cut out for you. The same principles apply that apply to socializing puppies apply to socializing an older dog, except that older dogs have ingrained habits that are harder to break. You must develop confidence in your dog by taking baby steps in socialization.

Armed with lots really yummy treats, like cheese or meat, work carefully and cautiously to encourage your dog to try new things and explore new things. If your dog reacts

Socialization

- Start socializing your puppy even before he's had all of his shots, so long as you keep things clean.

- The key to successful socialization is to keep it positive.

- Taking your pup with you as often as possible exposes him to all sorts of people, places, and things.

- Find a puppy kindergarten class and start working with a trainer when your dog's a baby—he'll be much better adjusted as an adult.

particularly strongly to something, and you feel he might inflict harm on you or another person or animal, work with a trainer or behaviorist.

The great thing about socializing your puppy or dog is basically provides an excuse to get out with your dog and introduce him to the world. You get to see him through others' eyes and be flattered by the compliments (hopefully!). Your dog will love being with you, which will make both of you feel good. You will be encouraged and inspired to spend more time walking outside—not a bad thing at all!

Chapter 4

Crate Training and Housetraining

Teaching your dog where you want him to eliminate and then reinforcing that message is a top priority in every dog-owning household. Nothing is worse than watching the love of your life trot off to your living room and, before you can even say "No," pee on your most expensive carpet. With a puppy, an accident may be simply missed timing; with an older dog, usually more is going on. Either way, it's an undesirable situation.

Always remember that dogs aren't born understanding that we want them to eliminate outside. In fact, puppies aren't even conscious of needing to eliminate. For them, when nature calls, they simply respond and go. An older dog should have been housetrained. If yours isn't, you have your work cut out for you. The best thing to do is think of your older dog as a puppy, and start at square one, just as you would with a youngster. Unhousetrained dogs of all ages must be trained to eliminate where we want them to go, whether it's outside or, if you own a toy breed and live in an apartment in the city, a litter box or particular corner.

Successful Housetraining

Successful housetraining begins with a schedule and boundaries.

Schedule

The schedule's important, because it lets you (and your dog, eventually) know what to expect. Dog eats, dog needs to eliminate. Dog plays, dog needs to eliminate. Dog naps, dog needs to eliminate. You take him out when he needs to go (even if he doesn't know he needs to go). He does his business—success! The typical times you'll need to take your puppy out to relieve himself include:

- When he wakes up
- After his first meal
- Before you go to work
- Before his lunchtime
- After his lunchtime
- Mid-afternoon
- Before dinner
- After dinnertime
- Before bedtime

Use these times to set up a schedule that works for you. (Check out Chapter 2 for a sample schedule that includes feeding, potty breaks, and training time.)

Boundaries

Boundaries help prevent accidents by confining your dog to an area he shouldn't want to soil because he also sleeps there and to a place that's easier

A baby gate helps establish boundaries.

for you to clean. The ideal boundaries are established by a crate, although a dog-proofed room like a kitchen or mud room secured with a baby gate can also do the job.

Why a Crate Is Great

A crate almost guarantees quicker success with housetraining. How? A properly outfitted crate serves as your dog's own "den," a place where he sleeps, plays, and possibly eats—not a place he'll want to soil. Crates are designed to safely contain dogs. They're constructed of chew-proof sides that are adequately ventilated; a secure latch; and, if you choose the correct size, enough room for your dog to stand up, turn around, and stretch out, but not so much room he can eliminate in an unused corner. Crates are also designed to be easy to clean.

A crate is not a dog prison. Never put your dog in the crate in anger and "lock the door." Never leave him in the crate for longer than a few hours at a time and, in the beginning, for no more than a half hour or so. If you use the crate as a place to punish your dog, he will not see it as a safe den, but instead as a very frightening place. He will protest being confined there by howling and trying to chew it apart, which could cause serious injury.

Getting Used to the Crate

As beneficial as the crate can be, you can't expect your puppy or dog to

SENIOR DOG TIP

Older But Not Wiser

A senior dog who has had impeccable house manners his entire adult life may begin to have unexplained accidents when he reaches his golden years. This can be discouraging for you, because they're unpredictable. Having accidents can be embarrassing and demoralizing for your dog, who can't help it but sees how much he's upsetting you. If this is happening to your senior, consult with your veterinarian. Often incontinence in older dogs has a physical cause that can be controlled through medication. Let your vet know if you notice any other changes while your dog is on the medication.

simply take to it right away. He must be made to feel comfortable and safe there. Put a soft towel or blanket in the crate—something easy to wash in case of an accident. Put one especially intriguing toy in the back of the crate.

Place the crate in an area where your family spends a lot of time, such as the kitchen or family room. The crate shouldn't represent solitary confinement to the dog—it should be a

Crate Training

Follow these suggestions, and your crate training should advance smoothly.

- Spend about 10 minutes twice a day the first couple of days just introducing your dog to the crate.

- Feed him a couple of meals in the crate.

- As he gets used to it, keep the door closed for longer and longer periods.

- Keep a highly desirable chew toy in the crate so he has something to play with.

- Play classical or soft rock music (quietly) to help calm him.

- Don't let him out when he's fussing, only when he's quiet.

safe haven.

When introducing your dog to the crate, leave the door open and, with a handful of treats, kneel down beside the crate with your dog. Toss a treat into the back of the crate. Your dog should go in to get it. Praise him for going in and out easily. Do this a few times, encouraging him to go in and out and investigate without feeling trapped. After a few easy ins and outs, as he goes in after a treat, quietly close the door behind him. When he turns to come back out, praise him for being in the crate, and pause a minute before opening the door to let him out. If he starts to cry, don't respond in any way and avoid eye contact. He'll eventually pause—at that moment, pop the door and let him out. You want him to learn that being quiet is his cue to freedom, not crying.

Using the Crate to Housetrain

Once your dog knows his crate is a good place, you can begin to use it to reinforce your housetraining. All this time, you should have been adhering to your schedule of feeding then bringing your dog outside to eliminate. Start feeding your dog in his crate with the door closed. When he's finished, open the door, put on his leash, pick up his bowl, and take him outside to eliminate.

Start incorporating crate time into the rest of your day, too. After eliminating and playing for a bit (or spending some time together training a new request), put him in his crate for a little while. Always take him to eliminate immediately when letting him out of the crate. He'll learn that a potty break happens when he's let out, which is a cue to hold it.

A rigorous schedule demands a couple of trips outside after the dog's final meal, and one just before retiring for the night. At bedtime, move his crate upstairs to the bedroom with you or have a separate one there. When you

For Dogs Only

If you have young children, they will probably see your dog's crate as another interesting place for them to investigate. Kids love to get into old cardboard boxes and fold themselves up as small as they can, then pop out the top. They may decide the dog crate is the perfect reusable cardboard box. If you allow this, you'll find you have a few big problems, ranging from the possible breaking of the crate (an expensive loss); to the displacement of your dog, who no longer wants to share the space; to the inability of the kids to leave the dog alone when he's in his crate. None of these are desirable. From the beginning, tell your children (and their friends) in no uncertain terms that the dog's crate (his private house) is off limits to them.

Housetraining Without a Crate

If, for whatever reason, you decide a crate is not for you, simulate the crate experience but in a bigger (more distracting) space. First, choose the space. It must be somewhere the rest of the family congregates. If it's the kitchen, use baby gates to block off access to other rooms. Baby gates work better than closed doors because your dog will be able to see you when you leave the room.

Set up a corner of this space as a comfy retreat of sorts with a dog bed and special toy. Then, as with the crate, review and stick to your schedule, so you are taking your dog outside to eliminate at every appropriate moment. If you won't be home to take your dog out as often as necessary, you

43

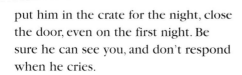

put him in the crate for the night, close the door, even on the first night. Be sure he can see you, and don't respond when he cries.

can hire a dog walker. If you won't be gone very long, but you want to safeguard against an accident, put newspaper and a pee-pee pad in another corner of the room. The pad contains an odor detectable only to your dog that will make him want to go to the bathroom there. The newspaper is there to soak it up. Clean up the mess as soon as possible after you get home, and clean the area with an enzymatic stain and odor cleaner so the smell of the pad doesn't linger.

You may find that the kitchen is simply too busy a place for your dog, with kids coming and going, meal preparation and clean-up underway, phone calls and business to conduct. See if you can put the dog's bed in a corner of another room where he can see you but won't be underfoot at all times. You could use an exercise pen (ex-pen) to set up a temporary enclosure. An ex-pen works like a doggy playpen. It's designed to be a temporary confinement system for your pup so he can't get into too much trouble. The pen can be set up inside or outside. Ex-pens are available at pet supply stores.

If you believe you aren't able to regulate your dog's trips outside

If you aren't using a crate to housetrain, you still need to stick to a schedule.

because you're so busy in the kitchen, consider attaching his leash to a belt loop at your waist. With him tethered to you this way, you will be more aware of signs that he's ready to eliminate. These include excessive sniffing and perhaps pawing at the floor, attempts to circle, or even hesitating to go into a squat. If you notice any of these things, go quickly outdoors to where you want him to go potty. You will also have more opportunities to do some easy training, calling him to follow you when you need to move around, asking him to sit when you're working at the counter or sitting at the table, and the like.

At bedtime, if you aren't using a crate, set up the dog's bed in a place where he can see you. Tie the end of his leash to something solid nearby. Leave enough slack in the lead so that he can get up and down and move around, but not so much that he can pace, paw at your bed, or wander around too much. You want the leash to serve as his "boundary" to keep him in bed.

The Spot and the Cue

From day one, based on the schedule you've established, when it's time, put your dog's leash on and take him outside. Have a plastic bag of treats ready by his leash for every outing and bring it with you.

Take him to a place where you want him to eliminate. Stay there with him. If

Eliminating on Cue

Believe it or not, it's not enough that your dog goes when you take him outside—although it's a lot better than an accident inside! Ideally, you want your dog to understand that he should eliminate in a particular spot, and that he should eliminate on cue. Sound like too much to hope for? It's actually very achievable because it's something you can "train" every single time you go out.

he goes, great! Make a big deal out of it. Choose a word that you want him to associate with eliminating, like "potty," and praise him enthusiastically. Don't worry about going overboard or looking silly—you want him to know he has just made you very happy. Say, "Good potty!!" and give him a treat, some petting, and more praise. If he's pooped, too, take him for a walk.

If you stand in the spot for longer than a few minutes and nothing happens, most likely your dog doesn't really need to go. Bring him back inside, but keep an eye on him. If he shows any signs of squatting or sniffing, scoop him up immediately and take him back to the spot. If he eliminates on the way to the spot or near the spot, that's OK. Say, "Good potty" for going, but don't be as enthusiastic as when he goes where you want him to.

45

Praise your dog when he eliminates in the correct spot.

you. "What a good dog!!!" Quick walk to stretch the legs, and back inside.

Another instance when this can be a lifesaver is if your dog needs to eliminate on unfamiliar ground cover. This could be on a city sidewalk when your dog is used to grass, or in a designated doggy potty spot at a dog show. How handy to be able to say "Potty" and have him understand that's what you want him to do.

The Bonus of Going on Cue

It's not so bad to take your dog out when it's sunny, but it's not so pleasant when it's raining, snowing, or freezing cold. That's when having a word associated with what you want him to do really comes in handy. With your umbrella in one hand and the dog on his leash in the other, go outside to the spot, say "Potty" in an upbeat, happy voice. If you've been doing the Spot and Cue routine, he should produce for

The Expert Knows

Don't Let Him Train You

You want him to pee and poop around the same spot, and you want him to do both fairly soon when you get outside. If he does, he gets extra time outside. If he doesn't, back inside until it's time—which may be immediately. What you don't want to do is establish a routine in which you go out, and you must take him for a 10-minute walk before he'll even think about pooping. He may begin to do this if you bring him back inside too quickly. Dogs love being outside and sniffing around. If you simply whisk him in and out when it's potty time, he'll figure out that he needs to stall you somehow.

physically able to cope—not to mention an owner who isn't particularly interested in the experience, either. Apartment owners aren't always crazy about getting dressed to take the dog out before bedtime when they could be sitting around in their pajamas instead, and an inside potty spot is a great advantage for them.

Indoor housetraining works on the same principles as outdoor housetraining: Designate a spot, teach the dog through positive associations what the spot means, and reinforce its use.

To get started, purchase some commercially available housetraining pads that you'll find in any pet store. They have a scent on them that makes a dog want to urinate. Put the pad under some newspaper and put additional newspaper around the area so that you are designating part of the room as acceptable for messes. Further confine the dog to this area by keeping him in his crate, or securing him behind a baby gate or exercise pen.

If crate training, when you bring the dog out of the crate, lead him to the concealed pad. If he does his business, praise enthusiastically and give him a treat, just as if you were taking him to an outside spot. If you're not using a

Use newspaper if you are indoor housetraining.

Indoor Housetraining

For young puppies, small dogs, and even geriatric dogs, it can be practical to train them to use a designated potty area inside rather than outside. This saves having to battle the elements of cold, rain, or even excessive heat with a dog who is less crate, encourage the dog to sniff around the pad, and praise and reward when he does his business on or near it.

After the dog relieves himself, pick up the dirty newspapers, put another pad in the same spot, and continue to lead or encourage the dog to the spot to eliminate. Gradually make the acceptable area for eliminating smaller and smaller by putting down less and less papers. Once the dog has learned that he has a certain spot in a certain room, you can introduce something like a doggy litter box for a small dog. Keep a fairly large area covered for a puppy or geriatric dog.

Accidents Will Happen

No matter how diligent you are, no matter how quickly your dog seems to be catching on, times will occur when he pees or poops in the house. Remember, he's just a baby. Even if he does it just after you've come in from a successful elimination and walk, he's not doing it to spite or upset you. This doesn't mean he should get the idea that you're not upset by his behavior, but be patient and keep your perspective.

If you are right there when your dog begins to eliminate, say "No!" sharply and scoop him up to get him

48

Accidents happen—don't punish your dog for housetraining mistakes.

outside. Picking him up will usually halt the flow. If it doesn't, hold him out in front of you as you head for the door. Carry him to his spot and say "Potty." He may not need to go anymore, or he may be frightened and reluctant. Give him a minute or so, then take him inside and confine him to his crate or by tying his lead to something stable so he can't move too far.

Get the paper towels and the urine and odor eliminator and, with him in sight, as you clean up the mess, say "Naughty dog. This is naughty." Speak with displeasure, but direct your scolding not to the dog, but to the accident. Throw the mess away, and take your dog to his spot again, just in case. Do not be angry with your dog. All you're teaching him by yelling at him is that you can be scary.

If you find an accident in the house, simply resign yourself to cleaning it up the best you can and to better confining your dog and/or taking him out more often. Do not drag him to the spot, rub his nose in it, yell at him, drag him outside, or do anything else punitive. Once he's done his thing, he's on to something else. He will not understand why you're upset; he'll simply learn you can be an ogre, and it may be wiser to avoid you. It's your responsibility to help him succeed, not to punish him when he's made a mistake.

A Must-Have for Dog Owners

If you think your dog's the only one having accidents, go to the pet supply store and see how many products are available to assist with and clean up doggy messes. A product you won't want to be without is a bottle of urine odor eliminator. It's an enzyme formula that removes the smell of urine and other tough messes like vomit and diarrhea. Besides doing the best possible job of getting rid of the accident, this product also won't leave the spot smelling like a doggy toilet, which often encourages repeat accidents. Choose the product you think will work best for you and follow the instructions.

Chapter 5

Getting Down to

Basics

As we started to discuss in Chapter 2, all dogs must master seven essential things to become well-mannered, obedient family companions. Those are: socialization, housetraining, sit, down, stay, come, and walking nicely on a leash. Now that you have a dog who's on his way to being housetrained and well-socialized, let's get into the lesson plans so you and your dog can build a way to better communicate.

When you see how easy and enjoyable the basic training is, and how your dog begins to respond to you, you'll want to get your whole family in line with what you're doing. That's important for two reasons: (1) Your dog will get consistent information from everyone, and (2) your family will learn, together, how to make specific requests that your dog will want to follow and understand. This results in a win-win situation.

Positive Training

What is positive dog training? It's certainly a phrase that is being used a lot these days. Essentially, it is used to differentiate teaching a dog through methods that positively reinforce the behavior you're training for and methods that negatively reinforce or even negatively enforce certain behaviors.

Not too long ago, animal training was considered an act of eventual domination or control over an animal. That control was achieved by sometimes producing pain to make the animal "submit." Choke chains constricted the dog's airway and pinched the skin on his neck, making him stop. When accidents were discovered, dogs' noses were held over them while the dog was reprimanded. And so on.

Today, trainers encourage animal owners to respect and understand their

FAMILY-FRIENDLY TIP

Kids and Training

It's to everyone's benefit in your family to know how you want your dog to be trained—what to say, how to say it, how to respond, how to troubleshoot. Training the family dog is not something that is done by one person; it's done by everyone. Getting the kids involved both helps them feel more connected to the dog, and empowers them by being able to successfully communicate with your dog. It's easy, too. As you come to understand how to train a specific behavior, like Sit, for example, simply have your kids watch you do it. Explain the steps involved, go through the process with your dog once or twice, then let them give it a try. Your spouse should get the same tutorial.

animals by teaching them with methods that give them pleasure instead of pain. Sit when I ask, and you get a treat. Come when I call, and you get a treat. Stay down in your bed while I eat my dinner, and I will share my food with you later. Have an accident in the house, and I will show you that I am upset by speaking angrily to the floor as I clean it up—all the while thinking how I can make sure you get to the potty spot I want you to use in time for you to use it correctly.

Another aspect of positive-based training is that it builds trust. If a dog doesn't understand what he's done wrong, and you're yelling at, chasing, or hitting him, how is he going to be affected? Simple: He won't trust you. For a dog who's rewarded and positively interacted with when behaving correctly—and whose needs are met—trust flourishes.

How Often?

If you think adding training the family dog to your already long to-do list is going to put you over the edge, think again. Training isn't something you have to carve out a time for and do in just the right way for 20 minutes straight or your dog will never respect you. Instead, it's a way to build a vocabulary with your dog and, as such, it should be enjoyable and easy. Review the instructions in this book to be sure you understand how to work with your dog before you get started. Then take about 5 minutes

before your dog's mealtimes, when you just arrive home, or during a coffee break to work on things like Sit, Stay, and Down. Using treats that get your dog's attention, a positive can-do attitude, and the steps in this book, you will have your dog responding appropriately with little "work" on your part. So think of the training not as another tedious chore, but as a fun way to spend focused time with your pooch.

Sit

Prepare to be impressed—with yourself and your dog—once you've

Keep training positive and fun.

done this a couple of times. And prepare to bring order into your life once your dog understands what Sit means. You can ask him to sit before mealtimes so he doesn't crowd you or scamper about. You can ask him to sit before going out the door so you're not dragged. You can ask him to sit when you must put on or take off his collar, when someone new comes to the house, and so on.

The Expert Knows

Clicking, the Ultimate Reward

Clicker training involves replacing the spoken "Good boy" that accompanies receiving a treat with a click. The click is emotionless and consistent, so for an animal who's been conditioned to understand that, when he gives the desired behavior he'll hear a click while receiving a treat, it becomes a clear signal. Many books and DVDs explain and illustrate how to effectively clicker-train and, if you're so inclined, check them out. Clicker training can be a lot of fun.

Sit Step-by-Step

- Begin with your puppy in his collar and on leash, and keep him in a fairly confined space that's relatively distraction-free (in the kitchen first thing in the morning, when the rest of the family is watching TV in another room, when the kids are doing their homework, or once you get the hang of it, any time you have an extra minute).
- It's handy to have your dog on a leash just in case he has trouble focusing.
- With a *really* irresistible treat in your hand (cheese, cooked meat, hot dog, piece of popcorn) let your dog know you've got something super-yummy so that his full attention is on you.

- When he is fully focused on you and the treat, and he is directly in front of you, bring the treat to his nose. Then, as he's working to get at it with his mouth, slowly lift it up between his eyes and above his head.
- Don't say anything as you're luring him through this.
- As his face moves up to follow the treat, his bottom will drop, and he'll naturally sit.
- As soon as his bottom goes into a sit, give him the treat and say "Good sit!"

"Sit"

"Yes"

Raise the treat above his head ...   *and reward when he sits.*

Troubleshooting Sit

Don't worry if your dog bounces up from the *sit* right away to see if you're going to give him another treat. If he does, that's fine. If he doesn't, let him know it's alright if he moves by using a release word such as "OK." You want him to stand again before asking him to get back in a *sit.*

If your pup starts to back up instead of dropping his bottom as you lift the treat, position him so that he will back into a cupboard or wall and will therefore need to sit. As you

practice teaching *sit*, and he understands that it's moving into position that gets him the reward, begin to move away from the wall.

Practice *sit* two or three times in a row—not more than that—and do it several times a day.

Practicing Sit

The great thing about this command is that you can practice it with your dog any time, anywhere. If you're in the kitchen making a sandwich, tear off a bit of the crust, put some peanut butter or mayonnaise on if you want to really entice your dog, and divide the crust into three or four pieces. Bring your dog into the kitchen if he isn't already following your every move, turn to him, and ask him to sit. Treat to nose, lift treat up, dog's rear goes down, "Good sit!"

Reward your dog with a small treat for sitting.

The *sit* is easy to work into your routine outside the kitchen, too. Ask your dog to sit before you open the door to come back inside your house after a potty break and walk. Ask him to sit before feeding him his meals. Ask him to sit before playing a game with him. When you're on a walk, ask him to sit before you cross a street. Ask him to sit when you come home—and don't pet him until he does! Each time he sits in these situations, let him know what a wonderful and smart dog he is by rewarding him with a treat or a genuine show of affection. Say "OK" to let him know he's finished doing what you asked him.

To make practicing in different places easier, keep small lidded jars of treats in different rooms. A small jar full of Cheerios by the front door, a small jar full of bite-sized dog treats in the TV room—anywhere you can think to practice and reward your dog.

Show your significant other, children, guests, neighbors—anyone you can—how to do this, too, and let them work with your dog. It's great for

him to focus on anyone who may reward him for sitting, and people who do this will certainly enjoy the results they get from his attention and compliance.

False Lures

You may have so much fun with this exercise that you accidentally train your dog to expect food just for looking up at you and sitting. That's why you'll want to incorporate some false lures into your sessions. Begin using false lures only when your dog understands the *sit* command.

With his attention still on you after having him sit for two or three "rewards," pretend you have another treat for him, put your hand in front of his nose, lift it up, and see if he sits anyway. If he does, make the reward a truly enthusiastic "Good sit!" and pet and praise him for being such a smart doggie. Incorporate a few false lures into your *sit* request in the future. By varying the pay-off by only giving treats randomly, it will help keep his attention, too.

Not So Fast

Don't be too eager to bank on the success you're having with *sit* and move on to train other requests. Rewarding for a few different things may confuse your dog if he doesn't completely understand the meaning of your request. For example, he may be sitting only when he thinks you have food. This is convenient—and correct—

when you do have food, but ultimately the idea is to respond to the spoken (or signaled) specific request, and not to merely offer a behavior to win the treat. Give your dog a few days or a week just to experiment and have fun with *sit*. Always reward what you've asked for with a treat or praise. Let your friend know you think he's *so smart* for getting it right. When you feel the *sit* is coming naturally, and he really understands it, start adding some new requests.

Stay

Stay is a fundamental request because you need it so often. Is your dog anxious to go outside for his morning and evening walks? *Stay* (and *wait*) will keep him from bolting out the door. How about when you go somewhere in the car—does your dog whine and excitedly try to escape from the vehicle as you're wrestling to get

Once Is Enough

Be careful not to allow yourself or others who work with your dog to be overly repetitive when asking for a behavior, even when you're in the early stages of training. A dog who hears "Sit, Sit, Siiiit, Sit!, Sit, Sit" before he has even done anything will learn either that it's OK not to respond to one word, or that your request is a series of words. Ask once, and expect compliance. To make this work, be intent and focused on the request, and use your "I mean business" voice (not to be confused with the "I'm getting upset" voice, which will not get you the result you're looking for).

MAKE IT EASY!

Teaching Sit

Here's how to teach *sit* as easy as 1-2-3.

- Use a tasty treat to attract and lure your dog.

- Hold the treat near his nose. Slowly lift it up between his eyes and above his head.

- When his bottom hits the floor (as his head goes up), say "Good sit!" and feed the treat.

his leash on? Asking him to *stay* (and *wait*) will make the process oh so much more civilized. Is walk time at your house an occasion for your dog to go running to the door and jump up and down? Teach him to *sit* and *stay* as you put on his leash. If your dog is like most, the joy of going for the walk will replace the treat soon enough. (But be committed: No *sit* and *stay* for the leash—no going out!)

Stay Step-by-Step

- Armed with a few tasty treats, and with your dog in his newly learned *sit* position (having just received his reward and while he still has his bottom on the floor), open your hand with the palm facing his face, and say, "Stay."

- Say the command firmly, but gently—don't drag it out or say it thinking it'll never work.

- Count to yourself, "and a one, and a two," then say with great enthusiasm, "Good stay!"

- Give him a treat as you say "Good stay!"

- When you respond enthusiastically and offer the treat, he will probably get up—that's OK for now, so long as he first held a *stay* for a few seconds.

- For the first few days, even a week if need be, only ask your dog to stay for a couple of seconds at a time.

- When you're sure he understands, begin to extend the duration of the request.

- When you're ready to add some time, make the request and, instead

The hand signal for stay *is the palm facing toward your dog's face.*

"Stay"

of counting to two or three, count to five or eight.

- If he holds the position for the extended time, reward with the treat and a heartfelt "Good stay!"
- Alternate asking for short *stays* and long *stays* to keep the training meaningful and successful.

Troubleshooting Stay

A common problem experienced with teaching *stay* is when the dog rises from position too early. If your dog isn't staying for as long as you'd like, go back and re-teach the concept. You'll only get a reliable *stay* when your dog really understands what he's being rewarded for. His objective is to get the treat (food or praise) as quickly and painlessly as possible. If he gets up too quickly, don't reward him. In fact, end the training session right there. He should get no feedback from you on errant behavior. Simply walk away.

Later, ask him to sit, then stay, and help him hold the position by keeping your palm facing him while you count to yourself for a few seconds. Give your dog the benefit of the doubt when you're re-teaching this, and only ask him to stay for a few seconds. Increase the staying time gradually as you continue to train.

Practicing Stay

A great time to practice requesting the *stay* is just before meals. If you've been working on *sit* all along, your dog

Using Hand Signals

You can use hand signals for all the basic requests you teach your dog, so you can eventually "talk" to him without speaking. The one for *stay* is to hold your hand flat in front of the dog with your palm facing him.

should almost be doing that automatically when mealtime comes around. Now, with him in a *sit*, as you're going to put the bowl down, stop, say "Stay," and hold the bowl for a couple of seconds. Then put the bowl on the floor with a "Good stay!" and "Good boy!" Slowly ask more of him in the pre-meal *sit-stay* until you can ask your dog to sit and stay while you make his dinner, put it on the floor, and turn away to rinse your hands in the sink before turning back and releasing with "Good stay, OK" so he can come for his food.

Plenty of opportunities arise to practice *stay*, especially in conjunction with *sit*. Add a *stay* to your request for a *sit* at the door just before you go out, before you engage in a game with your dog (hide-and-seek is perfect for this), when you want your dog to be still as you're getting ready to go somewhere, and other likely

Practice stay *before mealtime or before you go out.*

SENIOR DOG TIP

Savoring Your Senior

A dog who's slowing down can begin behaving erratically. He may seem disoriented, forgetful, and sometimes overexcited, as well as achier and stiffer. It's easy to get frustrated with your older dog, particularly when you think of him as the do-all youngster he was not so long ago. When you notice yourself getting impatient, take it as a sign that you need to slow down and spend some extra quality time with your aging friend. Take him to the park, go for a leisurely walk, and maybe pack a picnic so you can just hang out together. What a treat for both of you.

occasions. Having friends and family (especially family) make the same requests of your dog will only reinforce the behavior. Over time, your dog will simply expect to sit and stay for his dinner, before he goes out, and so on. What a good (obedient) dog!!

Down

Down is another request that should be taught only when you and your dog are enjoying the benefits of really understanding *sit*. This one isn't as easy to teach—or learn—as *sit* and even *stay*, so be patient. Going down at your request demonstrates real trust on the part of your dog. Earn it, don't force it. Again, an obedient dog is a compliant dog, not one who's been threatened "or else."

Down Step-by-Step

- With the tastiest of treats to entice him, lure your dog to you and ask him to sit.
- Praise him when he does, but don't give him the treat just yet.
- Kneel down in front and slightly to the side of him (ask him to sit again if necessary) so that he has room to bring his front paws down alongside you.
- Hold the treat at his nose—since you've been working on rewarding him for *sit* and *stay*, he will wonder why you're holding out on offering the treat.
- With his attention on the treat, slowly move your hand down toward the floor and out toward you.
- You want him to bring his head down, and then start moving his paws out so his elbows come down and land on the floor.
- As soon as they do, give the treat with an encouraging "Good down."
- Once your dog has reached the *down* position and been rewarded, release him with an "OK" so he gets the idea that *down* only means all the way on the floor, and not to the floor then back up.

Troubleshooting Down

Some dogs will stand up as their noses go down to retrieve the treat near the floor. Try to prevent this from happening by bringing the treat down slowly and deliberately so that he wants to stay in a sitting/squatting position. Bring the treat toward you from slightly off the floor. If your dog won't keep his bottom on the floor as you lure his front paws into a *down*

For down, *move the treat to the ground and your dog should follow.*

"Down"   "Yes"

Wow Your Vet

position, keep some pressure on his backside, so that he holds it to the floor, while continuing to move the treat out and away from him. When he's in the down from this position, make sure he holds it for even a second before giving the treat and saying "Good down!" Try it again just once to reinforce the positive experience, then end the training session for the time being.

Asking your dog to *down* is a request you'll need to practice with a bit more patience and resolve than *sit* or *stay*. Don't get frustrated if he doesn't seem to get the hang of *down* the first few times. Don't scold him, but don't keep repeating a request that isn't making sense to him, either. Reward him for any successful *downs*.

Practicing Down

Soon enough, you'll find all sorts of ways to practice a *down-stay* in the course of a normal day. When you're preparing dinner for your family, and you don't want your dog underfoot, lead him to his bed or a comfy spot in a corner of the kitchen, ask him to down, then stay, and he's instantly out of the way. If your dog likes to follow you around while you get dressed, sometimes causing you to nearly trip over him, positioning a comfy pad in the bedroom and asking him to *sit*, *down*, and *stay* while you get dressed is something he should be able to learn to do. Old habits die hard, so reward him for short stays while he figures out

Down requires a little more patience than other commands.

what you really want. If he gets up before you want him to, don't say anything, simply lead him gently back to the spot and ask again for him to *sit*, *down*, and *stay*. When he's successful, release with a very enthusiastic "Good stay!!" and an "OK" so he knows he can move. Give him a big hug and a treat if one is handy.

Come

Is anything more frustrating than being in a situation when you want—and need—your dog to come, and he simply won't? Whether it's needing him to come in from the yard at night after you let him out to do his business, asking him to come to you at the dog park, or even calling him to join you in another room of the house, the fact is that responding instantly to *come* (the first time!) can potentially save your dog's life. It's that important. And yet so few dogs respond promptly to this request.

Whether your dog is a pup who is just learning these essential requests, or whether you have a dog who is already a master at avoiding your request to come, you can eventually have a dog who is reliable when you call him to come. Like the other lessons covered so far in this chapter, this one must be started slowly and built up gradually, with success enthusiastically rewarded along the way. The bottom line is that if you

want your dog to come to you any time you call (and that should be your goal), he must know that *every* time you call you will shower him with something he loves. Because this is a part of dog ownership we all love, it's easy to do. Treats, toys, praise, a game of tug, belly rubs, getting to sit in your lap—all are things for which any dog would come running.

Come Step-by-Step

Session One
- Your dog should have his collar on, and you should work in a room with no distractions.
- Be sure to have an adequate supply of bite-sized tasty treats at the ready.
- When you're securely in the room, put your dog's leash on.
- Now that you're alone together in the room, lean against the counter and just watch your dog for a couple

Praise your dog when he comes to you.

"Good dog!"

Don't use the come command to call your dog for anything negative.

of minutes.

- When he becomes interested in something other than you, say "Rex [his name], come" in a high, happy voice, and offer the treat.
- When he gets all the way to you (not at arm's length, as if he's merely curious), give him the treat and say "Good come," then "OK" so he knows he can go do something else again.
- Realizing you have the treats, and there's not much else to do in the room, he may sit in front of you, lie down, or offer other behaviors to try to get a treat from you.
- Take a couple of treats discreetly in your hand and walk to a different place in the room. This should break his concentration and cause him to

go off and explore something else, at which time you call him to come to you again.

- If he comes right away, praise, treat, and release.
- Do this a few times, then take off the leash and end the training session.

Session Two

At the next training session, which could be later in the day or the next day, work with him in a collar and leash again.

- If he likes to follow you when you move around the house, do that.
- When he thinks you're going to go in the kitchen because that's what you normally do, stop in your tracks and say in a startlingly happy voice, "Rex, come!"

- If he turns to you, without saying anything else, show him that you have a yummy goody in your hand.
- If he comes to get it, when he gets to your hand, feed the treat while saying, "Good come."
- Then say "OK," and let him do what he was doing.
- If he doesn't turn to you, go in the other direction and wait to see if he gets curious and looks for you.
- If he does come searching, when he sees you, ask him to come.
- If he does, praise, and give him a treat.
- If he doesn't, don't call to him again. Simply ignore him and go about what you were doing.
- Go back to working in a small, relatively distraction-free room so you get the results you're looking for. He just might not "get it" yet.

Troubleshooting Come

For the first week or so, keep the distance he has to travel to get to you short so that he can't become distracted. The lesson is that when you call, he comes, he gets a treat and a hug, then he can go do something else. When he's coming to you this way 99.9 percent of the time, start lengthening the distances from which you call him. Put him on a longer leash (a 6-foot [1.8-m] cotton lead is great), and always call "Rex, come" just once. If you don't get a response, turn away from him, and start walking, even if you need to pull him to move him in your direction. As he's moving toward you, repeat the request and bring him in to you by holding out the treat. No compliance, no treat.

Another secret to a reliable *come* is to never have your dog associate coming to you with anything negative. This may make perfect sense when you're sitting calmly and reading about it in a book, but all dog owners know those moments of rage when they come home and find an accident, something special chewed up or, despite using your nicest, sweetest voice, there seems to be no awareness on the part of your dog that you even exist. That's when you want to shout, "DARN IT, REX, COME!!" The message behind that delivery is, "Look out, I'm mad." Your dog may submissively approach and cower before you, but he's learning that you are unpredictable.

Another negative association for your dog is when you call him to come to do something he doesn't like, such as having his nails clipped, getting the mud off his paws, or getting a bath. Go and get your dog for these chores, instead of using *come*.

If your dog has done something you dislike, and you need to have him near while you "explain" his transgression, or you want to do something you know he finds unpleasant, go and get him. Do not use *come* as a threat. Dogs do things because they're good for dogs. Coming to someone who might hurt them in anger or who wants to poke or prod at them is not good. Using *come* in this way erodes the foundation of trust training at which you've worked so hard.

Walking the dog shouldn't be an exercise in frustration.

Practicing Come

Practice calling your dog to come to you in as many ways as possible. When you let him out of his crate or confined space, call and reward him for coming to you. When you're going to get his leash to take him for a potty break/walk, call and reward him for coming to you. At mealtime, use some of his kibble to call him to you, rewarding him with some from your hand when he does.

Walk Quietly

Other training books might call walking quietly the "Heel" command. Trained for obedience competitions, this request is made when you want your dog to walk alongside you, paying attention to no one but you and stopping and starting when you stop and start. Because there is a huge difference between the precision and discipline necessary for the competitive *heel* and the reality of taking your dog for a stroll around the block or in the park, this book is going to help you teach your dog to simply walk quietly on leash. If you think this is going to be easy, think again!

Your dog's instincts to sniff anything and everything around him, and to give chase to things that interest him, are tough to train against. Puppies and dogs learn to pull, lunge, or plant themselves while we're walking them because these behaviors get them what they want—which is usually to get to

Seeing Is Believing

If you want to see something special, find a local dog club that's holding an obedience competition in your area. (Look on www.akc.org to find such events.) Go with your family, if you can, and without your dog so you won't be distracted. Watch people working at all levels with all kinds of dogs, and be sure to catch a class where the dogs work off-leash. You will come away with a greater appreciation of what people and dogs can do together.

an interesting scent as quickly as possible, to chase a cat or squirrel, or to stay where the sniffing's good. If you have a young pup who is already pulling you on your walks, imagine what he'll do when he gets bigger and stronger. Now is the time to teach him his walking manners.

Once your dog is walking nicely, you can take him almost anywhere!

Walk Quietly Step-by-Step

- Ask your puppy or dog to sit while you put on his collar and leash—it's harder to squirm and shimmy about when you're sitting.
- If he gets up while you're putting on the collar or leash, stop and ask him again to sit.
- With his collar and leash on, give the release command "OK," and head for the door.
- At the door, ask him to sit while you open the door, and only open it if he's sitting. (This will be hard for both of you at first, but it's a great habit to get into, and it teaches your dog to sit at the door and wait for what he wants.)
- Once out the door, ask him to sit again as you close and lock the door—you and your dog will only set out together when he's done what you ask.
- At any time during the walk, ask your pup to sit.
- If he does, give him a treat and a hearty "Good sit." Immediately start walking again.
- If he doesn't, stop walking and stand still.

- When his attention is back on you, ask again. (Don't say "Sit….sit….Rex, sit…Sit! SIT!" This teaches him you don't really mean it the first time you ask. Simply do nothing until he complies.)
- If he pulls, simply stop dead in your tracks until he doubles back and looks to you for an answer.
- Ask him to sit, and if he does, reward and move on.

If he's interested in going anywhere, eventually he'll learn that you're in charge of whether and how far he's going to go. You are going to feel silly and awkward doing this, but it will pay off in the end. Patience, practice, and praise!

Troubleshooting Long Walks

As with the other requests you've been teaching your dog, this one requires baby steps in the beginning so your dog can figure out what it is you want. With walking quietly, especially, it'll help if you remember how very exhilarating being out in the great wide world is for most dogs. There is so much to sniff and do, and your friend has no idea that you aren't as interested in the local lamp post as he is. After all, that's where he's picking up all the messages of the neighborhood dogs. It doesn't get much more interesting than that for your dog. You really pale in comparison on the interesting chart. So that you don't inadvertently squelch your dog's spirit with this kind of training, reward his compliance with a super-duper payoff. If he can walk quietly on leash all the way to the park at the end of the block, give him a warm "OK" when you get there and let him sniff in all his favorite places at his leisure.

If your dog can reliably respond to these basic requests, you will enjoy a special way of communicating— one that brings mutual respect and satisfaction.

Chapter 6

Beyond the

Basics

Now it's time to develop your vocabulary with your dog so that he has even more opportunities to "obey" you. Wait—did you replace "obey" in that sentence with "comply with"? If so, congratulations—you're tuned in to the fact that obedience is simply a consistent understanding of and compliance with a request. That's what we all want our dogs to do, and it is possible so long as we are clear about how we teach, respond to, and practice the request.

You and your dog should be doing well with the basics if you followed the instructions in the previous chapter. Are you using your daily routine as a constant opportunity to train your dog? If so, you should be finding that you are having many more positive interactions with your dog, and fewer negative experiences. If this is happening, you're probably wondering if—and how—to take the training to another level. The way to do that is to develop your vocabulary with your dog. Teach him some new requests.

Several everyday requests can make living with your dog more enjoyable. They include *wait*, *leave it*, *drop it*, and *shush*. You also can teach your dog some simple tricks that make training more fun, that you and your dog will enjoy, and that are sure to please and impress your family and friends (all while boosting your dog's sense of self in a positive way, too).

Wait

You may be thinking that if your dog knows to stay when you ask, why would he also need to learn *wait*? The difference is that *stay* is a more permanent request. *Wait* is useful for those times when you only need your dog to hold still for a minute or so. For example, when it's time to go for a walk, does your dog get so excited that snapping the leash on his collar becomes a challenge? One way to tame the pre-walk prancing is to take the leash in your hand, stand between your dog and the door, and ask your dog to sit ("Good sit"), then stay. If you've been training *stay* properly, your dog should understand that he shouldn't get up until you give him an OK or other release signal. In this situation, it means "Keep your bottom on the floor until I let you know you can move."

If you feel your dog needs the sitting time to relax a little bit, or you need the time while he's sitting to grab a bag so you can clean up after him on the walk, then a solid *stay* is worth requesting. But if, by the time you're ready to put the leash on, you have what you need and all you're going to do is snap on the leash and open and close the door, then *wait* may be more practical. *Wait* should mean, "Hold the position while I do something that will

Move on to more advanced commands only after your dog has learned the basics.

enable both of us to get on with things." The association in your mind should be, "Hold that stance for just a minute." The association in your dog's mind should be, "This means she's not quite ready, and I should be still."

So you don't confuse your dog, make sure he really understands *stay* and can consistently comply with your request that he hold his position until you release him. It helps to have the visual hand cue be part of your request. Ask him to stay, then reinforce the request by extending your hand palm forward and fingers together like a policeman directing traffic. You should be able to vary the time of the *stay* from 1 minute to over 10 to 15 minutes, depending on the situation.

If you're confident he understands *stay*, you can teach him to *wait*, too. *Wait* is most convenient when you're going through a door (so your dog doesn't barge ahead of you), when you're both heading for the same thing (his food or water bowl), when you want to put the leash on or take it off, when you need to check for traffic before crossing a road, and when you need to make the bed before letting him jump up and join you on it. Again, all these instances are appropriate to ask for a stay, too, but when *stay* comes to mean "just a minute" instead of "until I say you can move," it loses its effectiveness.

The wait *command may come in handy for putting on your dog's leash*

Teaching Wait

Plan to introduce *wait* at a time when you would normally ask for a *stay*, such as putting on or taking off his leash, or while on a walk.

Putting on the Leash

- Ask your dog to sit first.
- When he's sitting, and you have the leash in your hand, stand in front of him and ask him to wait, extending your hand with your palm facing forward, just as you would if you were asking him to stay.

- Come to him, attach the leash, and give your release word, "OK," with praise and a small treat, "Good wait!"

On a Walk
- When you come to a road or path you need to cross, ask your dog to sit and stay.
- Stand beside your dog and hold the *stay* for well over what you would expect from a request to wait.
- After a few minutes, praise profusely, offer a treat, and continue on your walk.
- The next time you need to stop, request a *wait* instead.
- First ask for the *sit*, then make the request to wait in the same way you would for *stay*.
- Stand by his side, look both ways, and in a matter of just seconds, give the release, praise, treat, and move on.

Troubleshooting Wait
You'll need to practice *wait* for quite a while before your dog really gets it. The important thing is not to let him get away with a sloppy *stay*. It's your responsibility to mean it when you say *stay*. Be sure he holds the position for as long as you want him to. In the same way, mean it when you ask him for a simple *wait*. Be clear in your own mind that *wait* means "hold everything for now," even if it's just for a few seconds.

Practicing Wait
Make teaching *Wait* fun. As you walk through your house with your dog and a bag of treats (so his attention is on you), when you get to new rooms or the foot of the stairs, stop dead in your tracks for a minute, tempt him with a treat, and say "Wait" while you remain motionless for 15 to 30 seconds. Say "OK," give the treat, and continue on. If you vary your pace by running across one room before you stop, or getting halfway across the room and then changing directions, your dog will think you're playing a game and change his speed to keep up with you. When you stop dead and ask him to wait, it'll become a focused moment for both of you, and one your dog will probably better respond to than "same old–same old" training.

Caring for Your Dog
In all that you do with your dog, remember that you are his caretaker. It's your responsibility to ensure that you're not overdoing it with him. If you want to teach him something that he just doesn't seem to understand, stop and think about all the things that may be contributing to the problem. Don't just push through it or get upset at him about it. Work *with* your dog and not against your dog.

Leave It

Use leave it *to stop your dog from getting into the treat jar.*

It's hard for us to remember or understand sometimes the power of a dog's nose, although he reminds us of it every day! Puppies, especially, are led by their noses to explore almost anything. Once they reach the source of "Good Smell," they quickly put it in their mouths. Some dogs never outgrow the compelling desire to put their mouths around anything that smells interesting, whether it's a dropped potato chip or trash on the street. That's why teaching your dog what *leave it* means can be particularly useful. It gives you a way to clearly communicate that whatever is attracting him is something he shouldn't put in his mouth.

Examples of when *leave it* can come in handy are when you're putting food out for a meal or a party. Medium- and large-sized dogs can easily reach food put on coffee tables, and many can reach the dinner table, too. Dogs learn that kitchen counters, high chairs, school lunch boxes, snack tables, and many other areas around the house are places where food is often available. Some dogs become obsessed with patrolling and often raiding those places. Repeated requests to *leave it* when your dog goes scouting—accompanied by giving him satisfying chew toys and treats in other areas—can certainly curtail if not cure your four-footed scavenger.

Teaching Leave It

Leave It is a directional request that requires your dog to stop what he was about to do and do something else. Therefore, the only way to teach *leave it* is to set your dog up to *take it*. Then, you can catch him in the act, cause him to stop, and redirect him to something else. It's similar to teaching your baby the meaning of "Agh!" when he reaches for something—he is startled and stops, giving you the opportunity to put something appropriate in his hands.

Beyond the Basics

SENIOR DOG TIP

Joint Support for Older Dogs

Dogs age at different rates, so it's up to you to pay attention to the signs that your dog may be slowing down. Some of the first signs may be moving more slowly, difficulty getting up or down stairs, or hesitation in getting up from the floor. All these are signs of aging (and possibly aching) joints. Consult with your veterinarian about the best form of treatment to help your friend. He will want to continue to do all the things he loves to do with you, including any tricks you've taught him. Just be aware that he may not be able to do them as repeatedly or enthusiastically.

To begin training *leave it*, set up a situation in which your dog will be extremely tempted by something. Put a small plate of cheese and crackers on the edge of a coffee table, or place a small bowl of popcorn on the edge of the sofa in the TV room. For training purposes, put the object of his desire within easy reach, so it is clear to him what you are directing him away from.

To prepare your dog for the training session, plan to put the "bait" in a room that can be closed off from your dog. Prepare the food, go into the closed-off room, put it where your dog can find and reach it easily, then leave the room, closing the door behind you.

Work with your dog in a collar and on a short leash (his 6-foot walking leash is fine). Put some pieces of cheese or hot dog in a bag in your pocket, too, so you have a treat to give him during the training process.

- With your dog on his leash and the food reward in your pocket, open the door and go into the room containing the food bait. (Your dog should find it quickly and easily.)
- As he moves toward the food, and when he's very close to it, say in a firm, loud voice, "Leave it," while giving a quick tug on the leash to get his attention back on you. The tug shouldn't be so soft he doesn't feel it, nor should it be so hard that it jerks him around. It should occur exactly as you firmly say "Leave it," too, so that the action of turning toward you is associated with the request to *leave it*.
- The moment he is turned toward you, say "Good boy," and offer him a reward from your pocket.
- Ask him to *sit*, and if he does, give him another treat.
- Release him with an "OK," and begin to move so he can again become distracted by the food bait.

- When he heads toward the food again and gets close, firmly but gently tug his leash while saying "Leave it" in a voice that indicates you mean it. Redirect him to you.
- If he complies, show him how happy you are by smiling and saying "Good boy." Give him a treat.
- Repeat one or two more times, but no more than that.
- After three or four practices, lead your dog out of the room, close the door behind you, and ask him to sit and wait while you take off his leash. Release him with "OK," and find one of his favorite toys for him.
- End the training session by giving him something he really enjoys. After all, he just overcame a huge temptation to do what you wanted, instead! What a good dog!

Troubleshooting Leave It

To troubleshoot this request, set up scenarios in which you can be there when your dog is tempted by something. Then, you can say "Leave it" while he's going for the food (or trash, or whatever) and follow the steps you've learned to get his attention back on you instead.

Practicing Leave It

If you have a dog who likes to lunge and grab for garbage on city streets, or

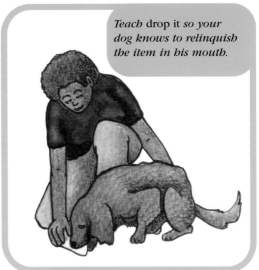

Teach drop it *so your dog knows to relinquish the item in his mouth.*

who is attracted to other animals' feces in the yard or while walking in the park, set up your "bait" in the yard or on the street. Always have your dog on leash while you are baiting him, so that you can gently tug him toward you and quickly redirect him to you when you say "Leave it." That's the critical learning for your dog: When you say "leave it" (and you must really mean it, because what he's after is very tempting to him), he should turn to you instead (and you should instantly praise and reward him for doing so).

Drop It

Drop it is important for the same reasons as *leave it*: It lets your dog know that the object in his mouth is one he should give up for you when asked to do so. The object can be a favorite toy you play a game with

A Drop It Warning

When your dog has something he wants in his mouth, and you want to take it from him, he may interpret what you're doing as wanting to play or, worse yet, wanting to steal from him. His response to wanting to play may be to run off with the object, causing you to give chase. A response to thinking you're going to steal his prize may be a warning snarl or even an attempt to bite. Either response is dangerous. If your dog acts in either way, you must stop your attempt to take what he has. If he wants to play, he'll have to come after you. If he shows aggression, leave him alone and call a professional to help you resolve the behavior.

should be something he doesn't mind giving up. Don't ask your dog to drop a special bone, for example, or a piece of toast—at least not before he knows what *drop it* means. Use a toy that he likes but is not particularly crazy about. If tennis balls are interchangeable for him, use one of those. If he has a not-so-favorite plush or squeaky toy, that will work fine, too. Don't use a shoe or sock or anything he really shouldn't be chewing on anyway, because allowing him to have something like that in his mouth sends a mixed message.

- Work with your dog while he wears his collar and leash, so you can best control him.
- Prepare a bag of small bits of cheese or meat to use as rewards when he does what you ask.
- Select the ball or toy you want to work with, and put it in a room that can be closed off before you enter it to train.
- Lead your dog into the closed room where the toy is.
- If he doesn't approach the toy himself, lead him to it, pick it up, and get him interested in it by shaking, bouncing, or squeaking it.
- Sit or kneel beside him as he begins to play with it.

together, like a tennis ball or Frisbee, a sock that your dog grabs out of the laundry basket, something suspect or even dangerous, like an animal carcass in the woods or a tin can from the trash. Your dog must learn that when you ask him to drop it—which means open your mouth and let me have what's in it—he must comply right away.

Teaching Drop It

When teaching *drop it*, the stakes can't be too high—what you want your dog to drop during the training sessions

- When he has a good grip on it, take hold of the object while it's in his mouth. Using your "I mean it" voice, say, "Drop it."
- With your other hand, get a piece of cheese or meat out of your bag and bring it to his nose so he can smell it.
- He should willingly release the toy so that he can eat the food.
- Protect the food with your hand a bit so he doesn't bite at it, but rather has to gently procure it from your hand.
- Give him the treat and say "Good drop it!"
- When he's finished his treat, interest him in the toy again, and repeat the process.
- If he drops the toy for the food a second time, end the training session.
- Leave the toy in the room and lead him into another room.
- Give him a special treat there (a few more pieces of cheese, for example), and let him have a different toy to play with or chew on.

Practicing Drop It

Continue to set up the sessions for teaching him *drop it* for about a week, depending on how well he's getting the idea. When he seems to understand, begin working with more normal situations. If you give your puppy a chew toy when you put him in his crate, ask him to drop it, praise him when he does, then give it back to him. If you're out on a walk, and he grabs something off the street, move purposefully to his head, kneel next to him, take the object, and say "Drop it." If you've been working on this, he should do it, though the temptation for him on the street will be far greater than in your house. Hopefully, you'll have a tasty treat you can give him in exchange. At the very least, praise profusely for his compliance.

Troubleshooting Drop It

If, while you are practicing *drop it*, he doesn't give up the object, don't force the issue. Take a few steps away and, if he still has the object in his mouth, stop and make the request again. This time you may want to be more insistent by pulling the object while

Practice drop it *with your puppy's toys.*

K-9 Delivery Service

When your dog learns what *drop it* means, you can also teach him to take an object (*take it*) and have him carry things for you. You may want to bring a dog toy upstairs but don't want to carry it. Ask your dog to take it, call him to join you as you go upstairs, and when you get where you want to go, ask him to drop it. You could even teach him to clean up after himself by designating a special doggy toy box that he has to drop his toys into.

firmly saying "Drop it." If this causes your dog to only grip harder, consider the opportunity lost, but make a note to yourself that this is something you *must* work on. If, even after doing elementary training to teach *drop it*, your dog clenches and won't let go, he is displaying aggressive tendencies, and you should consult a professional.

Shush and Speak

If you have a dog who barks at will, or who continues to bark long after an initial provocation has settled, you will love it when your dog learns this one. It will help restore calm in your household, help your dog feel better appreciated because you won't be frustrated by him so often, and may even bring back your family and friends who always have excuses for why they can't come over to your house. Well, maybe the last item isn't such a good thing . . .

Here's the ultimate irony about teaching a successful *shush*: First you have to teach your dog what *speak* means. Yes, that's right, you're going to reinforce the barking—but only at first! Once your dog knows that *speak* means "Go ahead and bark your head off," you can distinguish this behavior from *shush*, which means "Stop barking." Actually, a dog who already likes to bark tends to catch on to this more quickly than his quieter kin, because he already enjoys the sound of his own voice.

Teaching Speak

If you already have a barker, this part should be easy for you. If you don't, believe it or not, it may be challenging.

To prepare to teach *speak*, have some tasty tidbits handy, as usual when teaching a new request.

- No need to put a leash on for this one, but your dog should have his collar on.
- Get his attention with a tasty treat.

- By now, he will probably sit immediately when he senses that you're going to work with him to learn something new.
- If he goes right into a sit, get your session off to a good start by praising with a "Good sit!" and giving a treat.
- Deliberately keep a firm hold on the treat, and wave it excitedly in front of him. (The intention is to get him so excited, even agitated, that he will want to bark at you.)
- It's OK if he gets up and moves around, so long as you keep him focused on wanting to get the treat and getting him worked up enough to finally have him bark.
- The instant that he barks, feed him the treat while exclaiming in a happy voice, "Good speak!"
- Your dog may think you've completely lost it—a treat for barking?? So do it again.
- Entice him with a treat, get him worked up enough, and when he barks, feed him the treat while congratulating him with a "Good speak!"
- Try it a third time—if he seems to catch on, that's great. If not, that's fine, too.

Practicing Speak

Practice the *speak* when you and your dog are where either you won't bother anyone or where others will appreciate your dog's full-throated woofs. The sparkle in your eyes when you make the request (following the instructions above) should cue your dog in to what you're going to ask, and he should be happy to comply. As he begins to speak, encourage him by possibly "speaking" back. Have a woof fest.

Troubleshooting Speak

If your dog gets started barking and doesn't want to stop, simply turn your back to him and stand facing away from him, so that he is not being

FAMILY-FRIENDLY TIP

Seeing Is Believing

Teaching your dog the requests for *speak* and *shush* in front of your children is an excellent lesson for them. It reinforces the fact that there are times when it is inappropriate to be loud. After all, if your dog is expected to settle and quiet down, shouldn't the children be, too? You may even find that, having watched you train your dog to *shush*, your children may respond to the same request. If they do, "treat" them as enthusiastically, perhaps by doling out a small piece of candy for their compliance.

stimulated by you in any way. For as long as it takes him to settle down, simply continue to remain expressionless and emotionless. Turn to face away from him if he circles in front of you. When he has settled down, turn to him and calmly pet him to let him know that you are happy with him again. Wait a couple of minutes, and ask him to speak again.

Before your dog can understand shush, *be must learn* speak.

"Speak"

Teaching Shush

When your dog really understands that asking him to speak allows him to bark, and you can start saying "Speak" and having him respond with some regularity, it's time to teach *shush* (you can also call this command *quiet*). Don't introduce *shush* too soon, or your dog won't clearly understand the difference.

- Ask your dog to speak.

- When he complies, say, "Good speak" and give a treat to go with it.
- Now ask him to speak again, but when he does, don't reward him with a treat.
- He's going to think that's strange, and your negligence may cause him to bark at you to get you to give him a treat. That's OK.
- Simply keep the treat closed in your

Resorting to the Doorbell

If your dog won't respond by barking when you try getting him worked up with food, think about what might cause him to bark. Most dogs respond to a doorbell ringing or loud knock at the door. If yours does, ask someone to help you so you can cue him this way. Depending on your dog, you may need someone to do this a couple of times, but hopefully not more than that. Your dog should catch on that you're asking him to bark when you say "speak."

"Shush"

of kibble from the container and encourage the *speak*, and immediately after, the *shush*. Then move into the normal mealtime *sit*-and-*stay* routine.

hand and avoid eye contact with your dog.

- When you can see that he is ready to be quiet, look at him, say "Shush" in your "I mean it" voice, and give him a treat.

Practicing Shush

It will take a while before your dog makes the association that you have added a request to stop barking, so you'll want to practice this one fairly frequently. Before meals is always an excellent time to work in some training, because your dog is excited about the event and focused on you. If you've worked him up to a routine of sitting and staying while you prepare his food (which you should have), you don't want to interfere with that. So, about 5 minutes before your dog's normal dinner time, get a couple pieces

Troubleshooting Shush

If your dog doesn't seem to understand *shush* and wants to continue to speak, end what seems to him to be a great game. If you've asked for *shush* and gotten maybe a sideways look and another bark, simply end the training session. Walk away from your dog, put away any goodies you may have, and go sit down and occupy yourself with something else. If necessary, put your dog in his crate to help settle him down. (Speaking can be so much fun!) Try again later.

In Chapter 7, you'll read about how to solve some common behavior problems, and certainly excessive barking is one of them. Remember that old habits die hard, for us and for our animal friends. If your dog is a barker, it'll take time to work him down so he consistently responds to *shush*. You may need to change one of your habits in this process: Stop yelling "BE QUIET!" at your dog. The two of you may need to arrive at *shush* together. What a reward when your dog can *shush,* and you don't have to yell.

Shouting Won't Help

In frustration, many dog owners resort to shouting at their barking dog to try to get him to stop. They call out his name loudly and angrily, or they simply yell "Quiet," or "Shut Up." You get the idea. While this may startle your dog for an instant, it won't work to quiet him in the long run, or to teach him what it is you want from him. It may teach him to be (more) afraid of you, in which case he may direct his barking at you. This response doesn't work because a short, loud sound from you is similar to a bark from another dog. Your dog may interpret your shouting as trying to respond to him. It's a lose-lose situation.

Having a Few Tricks Up Your Sleeve

Few things are as much fun as watching someone's dog do tricks, from a simple shake to a wave, a bow, or a play dead. When you see someone else's dogs doing tricks like these, doesn't it make you wish yours did, too? Does a dog who's doing tricks ever look sad or scared? Usually, they end up missing a cue because they're so excited. And they tend to respond this way because they are experiencing what for them is one of their most enjoyable times: having fun with and

being adored by the "Love of Their Life" (that's you) while doing something simple.

It's time you joined the club of people who entertain and impress others by having your dog learn some tricks. Here are some practically fail-safe ones that can be taught to dogs of all sizes and ages. The only prerequisite is that you've done at least the basic training (Chapter 5). It's not that your dog must know how to sit and stay already (although that helps)—it's because your dog must understand your training methodology. If you haven't taught him that basic good manners earn him multiple treats, he won't understand that treats also come for unusual behaviors.

The tricks you'll learn in this book are Shake, Wave, Roll Over, and Dance.

Shake

Like *sit,* shake is easy for you and your dog to accomplish together, and oh, so satisfying when you've learned it. It's the basis for wave, high five, or any other sign you want to give your dog by meeting your hand to his paw. For whatever reason, dogs seem to think this is as much fun as we do.

Teaching Shake

- Cut up a nice pile of your dog's favorite cheese, a hot dog, or some cooked chicken, and let your dog see you doing it so he gets really interested.

- Take a few pieces, step into the middle of the kitchen, and stand looking at your dog—don't say anything, and don't do anything.
- By now, your dog knows the equation: handful of treats = learn new thing. But he'll also expect you to direct him somehow. Not this time.
- Your confused dog should be anxious about getting a treat, so he will begin to offer you behaviors to see if any of them might get him to give you something. (He will probably sit, which is great. He should sit before he shakes.)
- If he offers a sit, give him a treat and say "Good sit," then go back to waiting for another response.
- He will probably sit again, or if he holds the sit, he may lift his paw to solicit you for a treat.
- The moment he lifts his paw, extend your hand to meet it, give him a treat and an enthusiastic "Good shake!"
- Take a couple of small steps backward or to the side, to shift where you're standing and cause your dog to approach to get another treat.
- Again, wait him out—don't cue him, just wait to see what he does.
- If he sits again, this time don't reward him, although do make encouraging eye contact.
- If he extends the paw again—Bingo: Treat and praise with "Good shake."
- Repeat this a few times; your dog should get that you want him to sit and extend his paw to you.
- When he's doing that on his own, end the training session.

As soon as he gives you his paw, reward him.

Troubleshooting Shake

If you lose your dog the second or third time you step back and wait for him to offer you the behavior you're looking for, don't overly frustrate your dog or start sending him weird eye signals or making strange faces. Ask him to sit, reward him for it, then see if he'll put sit and extend a paw to shake together.

The ultimate goal is to have your dog do something for *you* instead of you prompting him to respond in a particular way. When you work this way, you make your dog think. He must figure out what you want. Believe it or not, this is really exciting for most dogs. When you respond positively and with food, and he knows that he has brought that about, he'll do it over and over (it's actually how most of a dog's bad habits form).

Practicing Shake

As you practice shake, progress to the point at which all you need to do is put your hand out and your dog will sit and give you his paw. Once he knows that's his cue, he should respond consistently to it no matter who asks. Have your kids get in on the game, your spouse, your friends, the people you meet in the street. Your dog will love all the positive feedback he gets for just sitting and shaking.

Wave

Teaching your dog wave is something that should be easy once he knows shake. Waving is simply shaking multiple times.

Teaching Wave

• Have your treats ready—already your dog will make the association that treats mean something is expected of him.
• Extend your hand as if you want your dog to shake, but don't meet your dog's paw as you normally would for shake.
• Instead, move your hand so that you cause his paw to miss it.
• Then move your hand back up in the shake (or slap me five) position, still not letting his paw quite reach your hand.
• If your dog keeps his paw extended and attempts to shake a couple of times, give him a treat while saying "Good wave!"
• So that you don't overly confuse him, go with a standard shake on the next interaction.
• Then, when he thinks you're back to "normal" and all he has to do is reach your hand, work on wave with him, keeping your hand far enough away from his paw so that he won't be able to reach it to shake, but close enough and moving enough so

Shake *is an easy trick to teach your dog.*

that he keeps trying.

- Multiple attempts to shake result in wave.

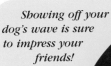

Showing off your dog's wave is sure to impress your friends!

- As he gets the hang of it, increase the number of times you want his paw to move up and down before praising him for a good wave.

Roll Over

This is a fun trick for you and your dog, but before you decide you want to teach it, think about your dog's overall condition. If he's old or overweight, he may have trouble getting himself all the way over, whether it's because his joints are aching or he's simply too heavy. If your dog is in good shape, though, no matter his size, he should be able to manage this one.

Rolling over can be exhilarating for your dog once he learns how to do it. Remember that it's a fairly physical endeavor. Again, depending on your dog's physical capabilities, he may or may not be suited to doing this too often. It's up to you to keep an eye on how he handles this one.

Teaching Roll Over

Rolling over is a series of three moves: down, over, and up. It is the most complicated thing you've asked your dog to do so far, so it must be taught in steps.

Step One: Down

- Ask your dog to down (Chapter 5) by using a treat to lure him into the position.
- When your dog is in the *down* position, take another treat and, keeping it close to his nose and mouth, move it slowly in a counterclockwise motion. To stay with it, your dog has to go over on his side.
- When he's on his side, which is about one-third of the over part, give him the treat.
- Repeat working with him on just going down and following a treat lure so that he lies on his side.
- When he seems to understand the request to go from a regular down to a side down, end the roll over training session for the time being.

Beyond the Basics

- You may want to finish up your training time with a request for a normal down, or short down-stay, just to reinforce the difference.

Step Two: Over

- The next time you want to progress with roll over (which could be later the same day or the next day; give it some time, but not too much), take your dog through the steps he should know—down and down on his side—and reward him for doing that.
- Then, with your dog on his side as you requested, instead of feeding him the treat for being in this position, continue to hold on to it. Lure him in a counterclockwise motion so that his nose moves his head (which will move his body) all the way over.
- Try not to physically help your dog bring his body over. The movement may seem awkward or uncomfortable for him, and he may simply get up instead of continue to follow the treat.
- If he does, don't reward him, just let him stretch his legs for a minute, and start over.
- Keep the treat close to your dog's nose and mouth, so that he is almost able to nibble on it.
- Timing is important here, too, and it is something you must feel out with your dog: Move the treat too

slowly and your dog won't get the momentum going that he needs to flip himself over; move the treat too quickly and he may simply stand up and try to get it.

- Whenever your dog gets to the point when he goes from down, to side down, to feet off the floor and over, make a *huge* fuss over him to let him know that he got it.
- Say "Good roll over!" as you hug him and give him treats. He may have surprised himself, and he will need the positive feedback.
- After a minute or so, reinforce the success by going through the motions again to see if he can repeat them.
- If he manages to go over even twice in a row, let him know how special he is and end the training session.

Troubleshooting Step Two

If, after several attempts, you don't feel your dog is getting it, or you think one physical prompt may make a big difference, go ahead and try to move

Roll over *can be a fun trick to teach your dog.*

his legs for him as you continue to hold the food lure near his nose and circle it over his head. Once your dog completes the over motion for the first time—at which point you cheer loudly and give him a few treats—the light bulb should go on, and the next few requests to go over should be easier. Getting to that first complete over can take time, though.

If he doesn't seem to get it after a few tries, end your training session by having him go to whatever stage he was able to accomplish, give him a treat without being too enthusiastic, and move on with your day. Come back to the trick later.

Step Three: Up

At the beginning of the discussion, I said this trick was a three-parter: down, over, and up. You will find that once your dog's feet and body go over, he will naturally want to get up. He should, and you can give him his treat when he's on his feet.

Dance

Dance is when your dog completes a circle on his feet. It can be on all four feet, or on just his hind feet. Your dog's own style will emerge as you teach him this trick, and he will determine whether he prefers to stay on all fours or bounce on his hind feet for you.

Dance is a fun request to make of your dog when you know he's really excited about something. Maybe you're

Roll Over

Rolling over can be simplified if you think of it this way:

- Your dog needs to know *down*.
- Your dog needs to be in good enough physical shape to be able to turn himself over.
- You must be able to maneuver the treat in such a way that your dog stays on the floor to get it.
- You need a sense of humor! If it first you don't succeed, try again!

going to take him on a car ride, or you're going to go play in the snow together. When you can tell your dog is just brimming with joy, it's great to be able to direct that energy into a dance.

Teaching Dance

- Arm yourself with some super-tasty treats.
- Start teaching this trick as you did *shake*, by moving into the middle of the room with your dog focused on the fact that you have something yummy. Then just stand there.
- See what behavior your dog offers you—it will probably be some version of *sit* or *down*.
- You want him to start from a *sit* position, so when he sits, reward

him for that—only once.

- Resume your "post" position and, without saying or doing anything, see what your dog does next.
- He should sit again, but don't give him a treat.
- When that doesn't get him a treat, he will probably move his paw as if to shake or wave.
- With his paw up, bring your hand (holding a smelly treat) straight up over his head so that he has to move his nose up toward the ceiling to try to get it.
- This may cause him to bring both feet off the ground. If it does, give him a treat and say "Yes!"
- If he follows the treat with his nose, but doesn't move his feet, lift your hand straight up toward the ceiling, slowly, to encourage him to put his weight on his hind feet and bring his front feet off the

floor to reach for the treat.

- If he does that, give him the treat and say "Yes!"
- After rewarding him for this initial effort, take a step or two back and start from the beginning—you're the post, waiting for your dog to do something to earn a treat.
- He should sit, at which time you bring a treat toward him, but don't give it to him.

Use a treat to lure your dog onto his hind legs.

- Hold it straight over his head so he has to reach for it, and begin to move it in a small circle so that he has to reach and turn.
- If he puts his front feet on the ground but continues to follow with his head and body, fine.
- Complete the circle. Say "Yes, good dance!" and give him a couple of treats.
- If he keeps his front paws up and begins to bounce around on his hind feet to follow, great.
- Complete the circle (or even a half- or three-quarter turn), and give him a treat or two while saying "Yes, good dance!"

Practicing Dance

Work on dance by continuing to encourage the circular movement from your dog before he earns the treat. He will come to associate a circular movement of your hand above his head with the request to dance. Reinforce that with a treat whenever you get the response you're looking for.

When your dog is comfortable moving in one direction, ask him to circle, or dance, in the opposite direction. Eventually, you should be able to move your hand in a circle clockwise or counterclockwise, and he will dance in that direction. Begin to choreograph a dance with your dog: Ask for a clockwise dance, take a few steps, then ask for a counter-clockwise dance.

Professional Doggy Dancers

A competitive sport called Freestyle actually pairs people and dogs "dancing" together. People train their dogs to move with them to a particular song. During the song, they do any number of moves, from the dog going between their legs to walking on two feet beside them to doing turns across the floor. It's amazing and beautiful to watch. Learn more about it at the website www.worldcaninefreestyle.org.

Using this chapter and Chapter 5, you should be able to easily teach your dog all sorts of things. As the world of possibilities opens up to you, the bond between you—and the obedience you're looking for—should be getting closer.

Chapter 7

Solving Common

Behavior Problems

On the road to "obedient," which you've properly redefined for yourself as willing and compliant, you've learned so far to teach and shape behaviors that you want in your dog. Hopefully, you and your dog have succeeded in teaching and learning the basics and a few other handy requests. The purpose of this chapter is to help you go beyond teaching and shaping behaviors to actually attempting to change those behaviors you don't want in your dog.

Change Is HARD!

What was the last unappealing behavior of your own that you tried to change? Did you try to quit smoking? Did you try to stop nagging your spouse? Did you try to cut back on how much sugar you eat? If you tackled any of these big changes— or even did something as seemingly simple as drinking more plain water every day—then you understand how difficult it is to change a behavior pattern: a habit. Habits are tough to break because you've been doing them so long that you're not even aware of them. (How about chewing your nails, or always opening the refrigerator door?)

Where your dog is concerned, his "bad habits" are really only your issues. He doesn't know he has them. You (and those affected by the bad habits) are the only one who cares. You trying to break him of something you don't want him to do, but he isn't even aware of what he's doing wrong, so he can offer you no conscious help to achieve your goal. At least when he's learning *sit* and getting treats for doing it right, he gets an idea of what you want and therefore what he should be doing. Not so with a bad habit or behavior.

A sudden change in behavior could indicate a medical problem—make sure you get your dog checked out with your vet.

Have You Created a Monster?

As his leader, his bad habits are entirely your responsibility—and often your doing. Did you think it was cute when he scampered over to you while you were eating and gave you that "Aren't I adorable…and starving?"—look? If you couldn't resist it, even once, and slipped him part of your meal, you— yes, you—initiated his bad habit. In his mind, he got what he wanted, without doing much. He will certainly try it again, and again. If he's not successful with you, perhaps someone else eating something good will share with him. Suddenly, he's a beggar.

Another example may be jumping up to sleep on the furniture. When he was a little bundle of fluff, did you cherish the times when he fell asleep in your lap while you were sitting on the sofa or in a favorite chair? Did you allow him to stay on the bed with you when your husband was away on a business trip—and now you find him on the bed all the time? The list of our dog's bad habits can go on and on. Some we decide we can live with, and others are simply too disruptive and sometimes dangerous to our family, friends, and neighbors to be tolerated.

Because they're your responsibility, you must figure out how to deal with your dog's behavior problems. Entire books are dedicated to some of the most vexing of dog behaviors, including some of reviewed in this chapter. This book can only give you an overview and a few practical ideas for solving your problem. Part of the work you need to do is "bone up" (excuse the pun) on the roots of the behavior problems you're dealing with. Talk to others who may be going through what you're going through. If you haven't done so already, find a training class with a teacher you can really trust and work with. He may help you save your dog's life.

The Expert Knows

Finding a Trainer

Just as the right coach can help you truly excel on the athletic field, the right trainer can get to the roots of your dog's issues more quickly, and better assist you in changing your dog's behavior. A great place to begin your search for the right trainer is through the Association of Pet Dog Trainers (www.apdt.com). The APDT is the only pet-dog training organization that offers certification for trainers. Its members are committed to positive, reward-based training methodologies.

Regaining Control at Home

Your dog's bad behaviors happen where he spends the most time—your home, yard, and neighborhood. That makes sense. Fortunately, because he's a dog and doesn't understand what he's doing wrong, he isn't able to argue with you or justify his behaviors. That gives you an advantage, because you can control his environment. You can control the things that are important to him: his meals, his walks, where he is allowed to nap, how close he can get to the kids.

Five things you can do at home can make a big difference in how he behaves:

1. Set limits.

2. Reward only for good behavior.
3. Don't respond emotionally.
4. Modify his diet or feeding routine.
5. Be sure he gets plenty of exercise.

Setting Limits

If your dog is allowed to go anywhere and do anything in the house—even if he's housetrained—he is one lucky pooch. Does he join you for dinner? Sleep on your bed? Initiate his favorite game even if you're doing something else? These relatively innocent acts let him know that he is on fairly equal footing with you. Confidence is one thing, but overconfidence is another. After all, would you waltz into your boss's office anytime and sit on his desk while he was making a phone call? Would you invite yourself to lunch? You get the picture…

What are some ways to set limits? Establish house rules and stick to them. Your dog should not make the rules. It will be hard for you to do this, because it's going to feel as if you're punishing your dog. Keep telling yourself that it's the only way to start seeing change. One thing you can do is insist that he stay in a different room while you eat. If that's simply not possible,

then he will need to stay on his bed or in his crate. The spot must be somewhere confining and separating, and he must feel the separation, either physically or by being asked to be better behaved. He may protest by pacing, whining, even barking. You would, too, if you were him. Tough it out.

Establish other limits by keeping him crated or in a small room set off with a baby gate. When it's necessary to leave the crate or room, put a leash on him and supervise him at all times. No more running through the house when he wants to. Limit his comings and goings to necessary trips: to the potty, to eat, for short periods of play.

Limit the number of people he can play with at any one time, and keep play as quiet as possible. Limit the

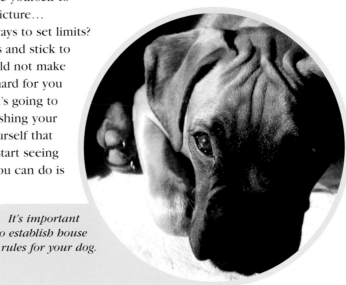

It's important to establish house rules for your dog.

length of your walks. Limit allowing him on any furniture until he's earned it. To enforce the "limit," be sure he has his collar on so you can redirect him when necessary.

Reward Only for Good Behavior

Rewarding only for good behavior is essential. Even looking at him while he's acting out to get your attention is a reward for him, so be sure you only respond when he's doing something he should. For example, when you are confining him to his crate while you eat, only pay attention to him for finally settling down, *not* for whining or barking.

Don't Respond Emotionally

It's important to keep your emotions in check when your dog is displaying a behavior you don't like. To use the crate example again, if he is barking or whining, don't yell at him to be quiet, don't sigh because you feel bad for him. To complicate things even further, your whole family must do the same thing. In other words, if your dog is in his crate in the kitchen whining because you are all eating at the table nearby, it's critical that everyone ignores him. If possible, try talking right through your dog's complaining. If it's not possible, consider making it "TV dinner" night and moving everyone into another room where you can eat more peacefully.

Just like kids, dogs crave attention.

FAMILY-FRIENDLY TIP

T.E.A.M.

This handy acronym can be translated as "Together Everyone Achieves More." In the case of setting limits, the whole family should become involved. By working with your family to reinforce the habits you want to establish to bring your dog under control, you help them see the importance of the limits. Chances are your dog's annoying habits bother everyone in your family (just as those of another family member may bother others). If everyone can agree that it's to the whole family's benefit that Spot be limited to his dog bed, they can more easily understand when similar limits are imposed on them, such as no jumping on the bed.

They're not selective about whether it's positive or negative attention. Yelling and scolding, while scary, is still attention. Show your dog positive emotions when he does something you want or like (that's easy!) and negative emotions only when you want to warn your puppy, as in a sharp, stern, "No!" Once you've gotten a response, deal

with the situation and put your emotions on hold.

Controlling Your Dog's Diet

Dogs, like us, are what they eat. Perhaps part of your dog's problem stems from poor nutrition. Are you feeding a high-quality kibble that's appropriate for his age, size, and energy level, or have you resorted to feeding him fat- and sugar-laden foods because he won't eat anything else? Consult with your veterinarian about the overall nutritional value of the food your dog is eating. If the quality is OK, next evaluate the quantity. Is he getting too much or too little? Both can make a difference.

How about where, when, and how often he eats? Puppies, of course, need to be fed several times a day. Adult dogs should receive two smaller meals rather than one big feeding per day. Pay attention to how much of his meal your dog eats in the first 10 to 15 minutes after putting the bowl on the floor. Whatever he hasn't eaten in that time should be removed. Your dog should have a healthy appetite that you satisfy with a proper meal. He should not be allowed to train you to feed him what he wants, when he wants it.

Exercise

Numerous studies have conclusively found that regular exercise is good for least a couple of times a week, such as dog runs in city or state parks or a beach that allows dogs off leash at certain times. Be sure to obey the leash laws, and always pick up after your dog no matter where you walk or exercise him. Once you incorporate regular exercise into your daily routine, you'll find benefits for both of you. The time it takes to do this is better spent getting fresh air and exercise than cleaning up a mess your dog has made because he's bored and anxious.

If It Is—Or Isn't— Happening for You

If you initiate the five things outlined above and do them diligently, you should notice a change in your dog's attitude. He should be more responsive and "respectful" (whatever that means for a dog). He should have a better sense that you are his fair, just, and honorable leader, and not his equal. Remember, though: Dogs are dogs. They are living beings who have needs. Don't misinterpret some bad behaviors as simple responses to too few limits or the need for attention. Some behaviors are rooted in physical problems that may or may not be obvious. If you have

Exercise is a great remedy for a bored dog (above).

What you feed your dog has an effect on his behavior and health (right).

the body and soul—a fact applicable to dogs as well as humans. If you think your dog's morning sniff around the property is enough exercise for him, you're wrong. Put on his leash and get outside with him, in the morning and at night. If possible, include excursions to places where he can run off-leash at

SENIOR DOG TIP

Getting Old

It's a fact: With age and additional aches, tolerance sometimes runs thin. Your normally approachable, huggable dog may seem unhappy with the kids hugging him as he gets older. His joints, face, even tail may simply be more sensitive. Before you label your senior with a serious problem, be sure you've considered his overall physical health.

a recurring problem that seems to defy your best efforts, speak to your veterinarian about it.

Targeting Specific Problem Behaviors

Although addressing some of the points above may be helpful in general, it's important to know how to tackle specific problems. Here are some of the most common dog behavior problems:

- Aggression
- Barking or whining
- Begging
- Chewing
- Digging

- Fearfulness
- Jumping Up
- Separation Anxiety
- Stealing food, clothes, or other objects
- Submissive Urination

The advice here is intended to give you perspective and guide you to at least a partial (and hopefully complete) solution. If it doesn't, consult a professional.

Aggression

Aggression isn't always a full-out attack. Usually it's more subtle—but equally dangerous—behavior. Does your dog bare his teeth at you when you reach for his collar to get him off the furniture? Does he stand over and guard his food bowl or special toys? Is walking him difficult because you can't trust him to greet other dogs nicely? These are all manifestations of aggressive tendencies that will probably lead to a bite incident some day. If you notice anything like this, take immediate action.

What to do? Certainly the advice in the beginning of this chapter about setting limits, rewarding only positive behavior, not responding emotionally, and evaluating diet are things you should implement around your home right away. Of course, reinforcing limits with an aggressive dog can cause the aggression to escalate. There's basically no way around it: Because of the potential for serious harm, it's critical to begin working with a professional. Pick up the phone or go online right now and call 1-800-PET-DOGS or go to www.apdt.com. This is the contact information for the Association of Pet Dog Trainers, a national organization of certified, reward-oriented dog trainers and behaviorists. Finding someone in your area is the first step; if that person isn't qualified, they should certainly try to refer you to someone who is.

Barking or Whining

The first thing to remember about barking is that it's natural and, for many dogs, it's quite enjoyable. For your part, when barking or whining aggravates you, try really hard not to "bark" or whine back—which you're doing if you yell at or plead with your dog while he's vocalizing in this way. The message he gets from you "barking back" is that maybe he should be louder, or maybe he should repeat himself so that you stop. Instead, teach him to bark on command using *speak* or *bark*, and to be quiet on command using *shush* or *quiet*. It's usually easier to teach *speak* first, while your dog is actually barking. Simply encourage him by saying "Good speak." Feeding him will necessitate that he stop barking to chew and swallow. When he is finally quiet, say "Good shush," and reward him again.

Begging

This a bad habit that is easier to prevent than to cure, so from the very beginning, when it's time for you to eat, put your dog in his crate or confine him in a room with an engaging chew toy to occupy him. Only let him out when you're finished. If you want to feed him leftovers, put them in his food bowl and incorporate them into regular meals.

If you have a beggar, start crating or confining him. Steel yourself and your family to suffer through the barking and whining for as long as it takes. Only release him from the confinement when he is quiet.

Chewing

All dogs need to chew. Accept this fact, and take on the responsibility of providing your dog with safe, acceptable chew toys. If he's chewing stuff around the house, don't let him loose in the house. Crating or confining him with the

Some breeds are more "talkative" than others.

Give your dog plenty of appropriate chew toys.

chews and toys you've selected will leave him with little choice but to satisfy his needs with those. If he simply won't take to something you think is safe and acceptable, keep trying until you find something he likes. Again, your veterinarian or trainer is a good resource for suggestions.

Digging

If you have a dog who loves to dig—and again, digging is a natural canine instinct and can't be shut down—don't fight him, join him. Select a spot in your yard or on your walk where he won't do too much damage if he digs. Encourage him to use that spot by burying something there that he needs to dig out. Praise him when he does. Set up a small sandbox in your yard where your dog can dig. If he's digging in an unacceptable spot, it's because

you're not supervising him or directing him to an acceptable spot.

The same is true for "digging" indoors. If your dog is scratching at the floor, he's probably anxious or bored. Put him someplace safe (confined), and give him toys and chews to play with. Take him outside for a walk and direct him to his digging spot.

Jumping Up

Your dog can't jump up on someone if he's sitting down, lying down, or otherwise confined. Enlist a friend or neighbor, as well as other family members, to help redirect this behavior. Put your dog on his leash, have someone ring the door, approach with your dog, and ask the dog to sit. He sits, you open the door. He doesn't sit, you wait until he does. When the person comes in, give them a couple of

Filling Hollow Chews

Make a chew toy irresistible by stuffing it with goodies like a smear of peanut butter, some soft cheese, or pieces of dog cookies. Stuffable rubber chews or even hollow sterilized bones all do the job. Clean the chew first, then fill with layers of treats, packed in fairly well. Your dog will work the chew toy to get to the good stuff and, in so doing, will develop a healthy chew-toy habit.

treats and have them ask the dog to sit. He sits, he gets a treat. He doesn't sit, they turn their back on him for a moment. You make sure he doesn't jump up by holding his leash. You ask him to sit first, and be sure he does. Then the person should turn around and ask him to sit, too. Repeat until the dog complies.

This is something you'll need to do over and over again until your dog can control himself. Even if you confine him when you're expecting guests, eventually you'll want to include him in the gathering, in which case he'll need to know how to properly greet the guests—by sitting and being rewarded for it.

Playing Too Rough

It's critical that rough play be settled and stopped immediately. To settle your dog when he's playing this way with you, stop moving or making sounds. Stand up if you're on the floor. Keep your hands and arms close to your body. Be a statue if possible, even if the dog is jumping up on you. If he is playing with others this way, have them stop moving and get up slowly, paying no attention to the dog.

When he has settled enough to physically handle him without re-exciting him, pick him up or lead him to his crate or room of confinement. Give a long time-out for this offense.

Play should only be allowed if it's managed. As soon as anyone gets overexcited, calm it down and stop it. Do some training with him when he's settled down, too, to reinforce that you're his leader.

Separation Anxiety

This is the term used by some veterinarians and trainers to refer to dogs who go crazy when left alone, attempting to destroy their surroundings, barking and crying uncontrollably, and otherwise causing

Good Behavior

Remember the five best ways to a well-behaved dog:
1. Set limits.
2. Reward only for good behavior.
3. Don't respond emotionally.
4. Modify his diet or feeding routine.
5. Be sure he gets plenty of exercise.

havoc. Other trainers call this behavior "fun," because the puppy or dog is indulging in all the things he wouldn't be able to do if someone was supervising him.

Anxious or fun, the result is not pleasant for you, and not good for your dog.

To combat this reaction, acclimate your dog to your comings and goings by (again) starting small and making the experience a positive one. Without making a big fuss over it, decide to leave the house. Put your dog in his crate or a confinement room with a favorite chew toy, turn the radio on to a classical or soft rock station (something soothing) and, without saying another word, pick up your coat, bag, and car keys and leave the house.

Walk around the house quietly, listening to or spying on your dog without him knowing. Give him a couple of minutes, depending on whether he gets upset when you leave or not. If he does get upset, allow him some time to settle down (a really appealing chew toy given on your way out should be enough; if it's not, find something more

If you don't want him to jump up on other people, don't encourage your dog to jump up on you.

Get professional help when dealing with separation anxiety.

appealing). If he doesn't get upset, but settles right in with the chew toy, give a silent cheer.

When he's quiet, and you've been out more than 5 minutes, come back in as if nothing has happened, put your things down, and quietly and calmly greet your dog. Do not run to him and smother him with kisses. Put on his leash and bring him outside, just as you would if you were returning from a longer trip. Let him learn that you come home and take care of his needs.

Do this a few times a day in the first days and weeks, increasing the amount of time you are gone from the house. Stack the odds in your favor by making sure your dog has something worth playing with, that the radio is loud enough but not too loud, that sufficient light and heat is available, and that you

have made sure he's comfortable and safe. If you're confining him to a single room, be careful about leaving anything around that could make an engaging but unacceptable chew.

If you feel that you've tried your best with the suggestions in this book, and the situation is not much better, consult a professional before you become completely exasperated. Consider working with a dog trainer and your veterinarian. Your dog may need a medication that could help with his nerves while training him to handle things better.

Stealing Food, Clothing, or Other Objects

Fortunately, stealing is a fairly easy problem to solve, because he can't steal what he can't get to.

Unfortunately, that means the onus is really on you. You must be perpetually on the lookout for what could be considered fair game: accessible garbage cans, food left anywhere within reach, open closet doors. Make the inappropriate objects of his desire inaccessible while at the same time providing plenty of appropriate chews and other toys. Play with your dog using those toys, so the pleasure for him is in only using them.

When he does steal, don't chase him, or you're initiating a game. Call him to you or go after him methodically and unemotionally until you can hold him. Tell him "Leave it" as you open his mouth to remove the object. Be careful while doing this; if you sense your dog is getting overly aggressive, leave him. Confine him at the earliest opportunity and commit to working with an experienced dog trainer or behaviorist. The last thing you want is a dog to turn on you over a stolen object.

Submissive Urination

When you come inside to greet your dog, does he flop down and begin to wet himself? If so, you have a submissive urinator. First, be sure the

problem isn't due to a health issue. If it's not, confine him somewhere that's easy to clean so you're not doubly frustrated by a soiled carpet.

Crate your dog or put him in a safe, confined space. When you approach to greet him after being away for a bit, do so in as emotionless a way as possible. If the problem has been going on for a while, you probably approach him reluctantly, anxiously, or suspiciously. He can pick up on your feelings, and they can contribute to his own anxiousness. Pretend he's a strange dog who you must get out the door calmly and gently, but as quickly as possible, so he can do his business outside.

If he urinates as you're going outside, don't react. Stay the course to

Patient training and good leadership are the way to a happy dog.

Finding and Choosing a Behaviorist

How is an animal behaviorist different from an animal trainer? The difference is in the degree of education and certification the person has received in the study of animal behavior. The Animal Behavior Society awards two levels of certification for people who would be called Animal Behaviorists—an Associate Applied Animal Behaviorist, and an Applied Animal Behaviorist. Both require extensive education, experience, and professional endorsement.

On a more accessible level for dog trainers, the Association of Pet Dog Trainers (APDT) created a professional testing program to provide both a credible means of measuring their own knowledge and a credible barometer for the public to use when choosing a trainer. The Certification Council for Pet Dog Trainers awards CPDT designations to trainers who pass their rigorous testing.

You can find behaviorists and CPDTs through the APDT at www.apdt.com.

the outside, let him do his thing, confine him again while you clean up, and then get on with the rest of your day. You must respond as unemotionally as possible until you feel you're making progress. Slow and steady….

Final Thoughts

When training your dog—whether it's to learn a new behavior or modify an existing behavior—it's important to remember that he is an individual. The advice in this book may have worked for many dogs and their owners, but may not work for your dog and you. Explore other sources (see the Resources section at the end of the book for suggestions). Talk to other dog owners, particularly those who own the same breed. Observe your dog as objectively as possible when trying to determine the source of problems so you can understand what might be triggering them. Involve everyone in your household in the game plan to try to solve problems. And last, but not least, don't let good intentions keep you from doing what's necessary: If you aren't succeeding, but know something must be done, seek professional help. Don't push your dog to the point at which you end up condemning him to a shelter. Help your best friend with all the resources available to you. Your responsibility toward him will be rewarded with his love and trust.

Resources

Associations and Organizations

Breed Clubs

American Kennel Club (AKC)
5580 Centerview Drive
Raleigh, NC 27606
Telephone: (919) 233-9767
Fax: (919) 233-3627
E-mail: info@akc.org
www.akc.org

Canadian Kennel Club (CKC)
89 Skyway Avenue, Suite 100
Etobicoke, Ontario M9W 6R4
Telephone: (416) 675-5511
Fax: (416) 675-6506
E-mail: information@ckc.ca
www.ckc.ca

Federation Cynologique Internationale (FCI)
Secretariat General de la FCI
Place Albert 1er, 13
B – 6530 Thuin
Belqique
www.fci.be

The Kennel Club
1 Clarges Street
London
W1J 8AB
Telephone: 0870 606 6750
Fax: 0207 518 1058
www.the-kennel-club.org.uk

United Kennel Club (UKC)
100 E. Kilgore Road
Kalamazoo, MI 49002-5584
Telephone: (269) 343-9020
Fax: (269) 343-7037
E-mail: pbickell@ukcdogs.com
www.ukcdogs.com

Pet Sitters

National Association of Professional Pet Sitters
15000 Commerce Parkway,
Suite C
Mt. Laurel, New Jersey 08054
Telephone: (856) 439-0324
Fax: (856) 439-0525
E-mail: napps@ahint.com
www.petsitters.org

Pet Sitters International
201 East King Street
King, NC 27021-9161
Telephone: (336) 983-9222
Fax: (336) 983-5266
E-mail: info@petsit.com
www.petsit.com

Rescue Organizations and Animal Welfare Groups

American Humane Association (AHA)
63 Inverness Drive East
Englewood, CO 80112
Telephone: (303) 792-9900
Fax: 792-5333
www.americanhumane.org

American Society for the Prevention of Cruelty to Animals (ASPCA)
424 E. 92nd Street
New York, NY 10128-6804
Telephone: (212) 876-7700
www.aspca.org

Royal Society for the Prevention of Cruelty to Animals (RSPCA)
Telephone: 0870 3335 999
Fax: 0870 7530 284
www.rspca.org.uk

The Humane Society of the United States (HSUS)
2100 L Street, NW
Washington DC 20037
Telephone: (202) 452-1100
www.hsus.org

Sports

International Agility Link (IAL)
Global Administrator: Steve Drinkwater
E-mail: yunde@powerup.au
www.agilityclick.com/~ial

North American Dog Agility Council
11522 South Hwy 3
Cataldo, ID 83810
www.nadac.com

United States Dog Agility Association
P.O. Box 850955
Richardson, TX 75085-0955
Telephone: (972) 487-2200
www.usdaa.com

Therapy

Delta Society
875 124th Ave NE, Suite 101
Bellevue, WA 98005
Telephone: (425) 226-7357
Fax: (425) 235-1076
E-mail: info@deltasociety.org
www.deltasociety.org

Therapy Dogs Incorporated
PO Box 5868
Cheyenne, WY 82003
Telephone: (877) 843-7364
E-mail: therdog@sisna.com
www.therapydogs.com

Therapy Dogs International (TDI)
88 Bartley Road
Flanders, NJ 07836
Telephone: (973) 252-9800
Fax: (973) 252-7171
E-mail: tdi@gti.net
www.tdi-dog.org

Training

Association of Pet Dog Trainers (APDT)
150 Executive Center Drive Box 35
Greenville, SC 29615
Telephone: (800) PET-DOGS
Fax: (864) 331-0767
E-mail: information@apdt.com
www.apdt.com

National Association of Dog Obedience Instructors
PMB 369
729 Grapevine Hwy.
Hurst, TX 76054-2085
www.nadoi.org

Veterinary and Health Resources

Academy of Veterinary Homeopathy (AVH)
P.O. Box 9280
Wilmington, DE 19809
Telephone: (866) 652-1590
Fax: (866) 652-1590
E-mail: office@TheAVH.org
www.theavh.org

American Academy of Veterinary Acupuncture (AAVA)
100 Roscommon Drive, Suite 320
Middletown, CT 06457
Telephone: (860) 635-6300
Fax: (860) 635-6400
E-mail: office@aava.org
www.aava.org

American Animal Hospital Association (AAHA)
P.O. Box 150899
Denver, CO 80215-0899
Telephone: (303) 986-2800
Fax: (303) 986-1700
E-mail: info@aahanet.org
www.aahanet.org/index.cfm

American College of Veterinary Internal Medicine (ACVIM)
1997 Wadsworth Blvd., Suite A
Lakewood, CO 80214-5293
Telephone: (800) 245-9081
Fax: (303) 231-0880
Email: ACVIM@ACVIM.org
www.acvim.org

American College of Veterinary Ophthalmologists (ACVO)
P.O. Box 1311
Meridian, Idaho 83860
Telephone: (208) 466-7624
Fax: (208) 466-7693
E-mail: office@acvo.com
www.acvo.com

American Holistic Veterinary Medical Association (AHVMA)
2218 Old Emmorton Road
Bel Air, MD 21015
Telephone: (410) 569-0795
Fax: (410) 569-2346
E-mail: office@ahvma.org
www.ahvma.org

American Veterinary Medical Association (AVMA)
1931 North Meacham Road – Suite 100
Schaumburg, IL 60173
Telephone: (847) 925-8070
Fax: (847) 925-1329
E-mail: avmainfo@avma.org
www.avma.org

ASPCA Animal Poison Control Center
1717 South Philo Road, Suite 36
Urbana, IL 61802
Telephone: (888) 426-4435
www.aspca.org

British Veterinary Association (BVA)
7 Mansfield Street
London
W1G 9NQ
Telephone: 020 7636 6541
Fax: 020 7436 2970
E-mail: bvahq@bva.co.uk
www.bva.co.uk

Canine Eye Registration Foundation (CERF)
VMDB/CERF
1248 Lynn Hall
625 Harrison St.
Purdue University
West Lafayette, IN 47907-2026
Telephone: (765) 494-8179
E-mail: CERF@vmbd.org
www.vmdb.org

Orthopedic Foundation for Animals (OFA)
2300 NE Nifong Blvd
Columbus, Missouri 65201-3856
Telephone: (573) 442-0418
Fax: (573) 875-5073
Email: ofa@offa.org
www.offa.org

Index

Index

Dedication

First, I dedicate this book to all the dogs in my life who taught me, each in their own way, that there is no greater gift than canine companionship. Charlie, Wylen, Griffon, Ingo, Ziggy & Zola, Whiskey, Exley, Chelsea, Cinderella, and my dear sweet Chief, you are all in my heart forever. Second, to my family — Carlo, Dawson, and Dylan. Thank goodness we're all a little dog-crazy! To my mother, who was so right when she said, "Dogs don't ask to come to us. It's our job to take care of them." And I dedicate this book to Ian Dunbar, my earliest, and truest, inspiration for training dogs. He revolutionized my thinking and turned me on to what was possible for relationships with dogs and all beings. How fortunate for me that I was able to learn from the best.

About the Author

Dominique De Vito has been involved in pet publishing for over 10 years. A member of the Association of Pet Dog Trainers and the Dog Writers Association of America, she is currently a freelance editor and writer who lives with her husband, three dogs, and twin boys in New Jersey and New York state.

Photo Credits